Improve Operation
Complete Self-Assessment Guide

C000021057

The guidance in this Self-Assessment is base
best practices and standards in business pro
and quality management. The guidance is also based on the proïessiunaï
judgment of the individual collaborators listed in the Acknowledgments.

Notice of rights

**You are licensed to use the Self-Assessment contents in your
presentations and materials for internal use and customers
without asking us - we are here to help.**

Trademarks

Table of Contents

About The Art of Service

The Art of Service, Business Process Architects since 2000, is dedicated to helping stakeholders achieve excellence.

Defining, designing, creating, and implementing a process to solve a stakeholders challenge or meet an objective is the most valuable role... In EVERY group, company, organization and department.

Unless you're talking a one-time, single-use project, there should be a process. Whether that process is managed and implemented by humans, AI, or a combination of the two, it needs to be designed by someone with a complex enough perspective to ask the right questions.

Someone capable of asking the right questions and step back and say, 'What are we really trying to accomplish here? And is there a different way to look at it?'

With The Art of Service's Standard Requirements Self-Assessments, we empower people who can do just that — whether their title is marketer, entrepreneur, manager, salesperson, consultant, Business Process Manager, executive assistant, IT Manager, CIO etc... —they are the people who rule the future. They are people who watch the process as it happens, and ask the right questions to make the process work better.

Contact us when you need any support with this Self-Assessment and any help with templates, blue-prints and examples of standard documents you might need:

http://theartofservice.com
service@theartofservice.com

Acknowledgments

This checklist was developed under the auspices of The Art of Service, chaired by Gerardus Blokdyk.

Representatives from several client companies participated in the preparation of this Self-Assessment.

In addition, we are thankful for the design and printing services provided.

Included Resources - how to access

Included with your purchase of the book is the Improve Operation Self-Assessment Spreadsheet Dashboard which contains all questions and Self-Assessment areas and auto-generates insights, graphs, and project RACI planning - all with examples to get you started right away.

How? Simply send an email to
access@theartofservice.com
with this books' title in the subject to get the Improve Operation Self Assessment Tool right away.

You will receive the following contents with New and Updated specific criteria:

• The latest quick edition of the book in PDF

• The latest complete edition of the book in PDF, which criteria correspond to the criteria in...

• The Self-Assessment Excel Dashboard, and...

• Example pre-filled Self-Assessment Excel Dashboard to get familiar with results generation

• In-depth specific Checklists covering the topic

• Project management checklists and templates to assist with implementation

INCLUDES LIFETIME SELF ASSESSMENT UPDATES

Every self assessment comes with Lifetime Updates and Lifetime Free Updated Books. Lifetime Updates is an industry-first feature which allows you to receive verified self assessment updates, ensuring you always have the most accurate information at your fingertips.

Get it now- you will be glad you did - do it now, before you forget.

Send an email to **access@theartofservice.com** with this books' title in the subject to get the Improve Operation Self Assessment Tool right away.

Your feedback is invaluable to us

If you recently bought this book, we would love to hear from you! You can do this by writing a review on amazon (or the online store where you purchased this book) about your last purchase! As part of our continual service improvement process, we love to hear real client experiences and feedback.

How does it work?
To post a review on Amazon, just log in to your account and click on the Create Your Own Review button (under Customer Reviews) of the relevant product page. You can find examples of product reviews in Amazon. If you purchased from another online store, simply follow their procedures.

What happens when I submit my review?
Once you have submitted your review, send us an email at review@theartofservice.com with the link to your review so we can properly thank you for your feedback.

Purpose of this Self-Assessment

This Self-Assessment has been developed to improve understanding of the requirements and elements of Improve Operation, based on best practices and standards in business process architecture, design and quality management.

It is designed to allow for a rapid Self-Assessment to determine how closely existing management practices and procedures correspond to the elements of the Self-Assessment.

The criteria of requirements and elements of Improve Operation have been rephrased in the format of a Self-Assessment questionnaire, with a seven-criterion scoring system, as explained in this document.

In this format, even with limited background knowledge of

Improve Operation, a manager can quickly review existing operations to determine how they measure up to the standards. This in turn can serve as the starting point of a 'gap analysis' to identify management tools or system elements that might usefully be implemented in the organization to help improve overall performance.

How to use the Self-Assessment

On the following pages are a series of questions to identify to what extent your Improve Operation initiative is complete in comparison to the requirements set in standards.

To facilitate answering the questions, there is a space in front of each question to enter a score on a scale of '1' to '5'.

1 Strongly Disagree

2 Disagree

3 Neutral

4 Agree

5 Strongly Agree

Read the question and rate it with the following in front of mind:

**'In my belief,
the answer to this question is clearly defined'.**

There are two ways in which you can choose to interpret this statement;
1. how aware are you that the answer to the question is clearly defined
2. for more in-depth analysis you can choose to gather

evidence and confirm the answer to the question. This obviously will take more time, most Self-Assessment users opt for the first way to interpret the question and dig deeper later on based on the outcome of the overall Self-Assessment.

A score of '1' would mean that the answer is not clear at all, where a '5' would mean the answer is crystal clear and defined. Leave emtpy when the question is not applicable or you don't want to answer it, you can skip it without affecting your score. Write your score in the space provided.

After you have responded to all the appropriate statements in each section, compute your average score for that section, using the formula provided, and round to the nearest tenth. Then transfer to the corresponding spoke in the Improve Operation Scorecard on the second next page of the Self-Assessment.

Your completed Improve Operation Scorecard will give you a clear presentation of which Improve Operation areas need attention.

Improve Operation Scorecard Example

Example of how the finalized Scorecard can look like:

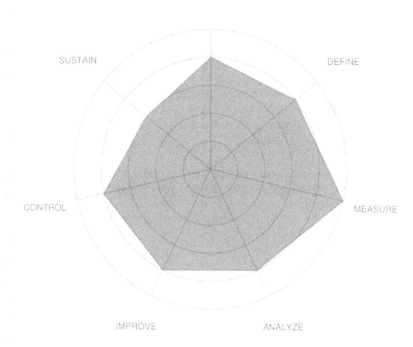

Improve Operation Scorecard

Your Scores:

BEGINNING OF THE SELF-ASSESSMENT:

CRITERION #1: RECOGNIZE

INTENT: Be aware of the need for change. Recognize that there is an unfavorable variation, problem or symptom.

In my belief, the answer to this question is clearly defined:

5 Strongly Agree

4 Agree

3 Neutral

2 Disagree

1 Strongly Disagree

1. What would happen if Improve Operation weren't done?
<--- Score

2. Who are your key stakeholders who need to sign off?
<--- Score

3. What Improve Operation capabilities do you need?

<--- Score

4. What resources or support might you need?
<--- Score

5. Are your goals realistic? Do you need to redefine your problem? Perhaps the problem has changed or maybe you have reached your goal and need to set a new one?
<--- Score

6. Are controls defined to recognize and contain problems?
<--- Score

7. What is the recognized need?
<--- Score

8. What Improve Operation events should you attend?
<--- Score

9. Where do you need to exercise leadership?
<--- Score

10. Looking at each person individually – does every one have the qualities which are needed to work in this group?
<--- Score

11. Which issues are too important to ignore?
<--- Score

12. Will new equipment/products be required to facilitate Improve Operation delivery, for example is new software needed?
<--- Score

13. How do you assess your Improve Operation workforce capability and capacity needs, including skills, competencies, and staffing levels?
<--- Score

14. Where is training needed?
<--- Score

15. When a Improve Operation manager recognizes a problem, what options are available?
<--- Score

16. How do you identify the kinds of information that you will need?
<--- Score

17. Will Improve Operation deliverables need to be tested and, if so, by whom?
<--- Score

18. What are the expected benefits of Improve Operation to the stakeholder?
<--- Score

19. How do you identify subcontractor relationships?
<--- Score

20. Do you know what you need to know about Improve Operation?
<--- Score

21. What is the Improve Operation problem definition? What do you need to resolve?
<--- Score

22. Consider your own Improve Operation project, what types of organizational problems do you think might be causing or affecting your problem, based on the work done so far?
<--- Score

23. Is it needed?
<--- Score

24. Are employees recognized for desired behaviors?
<--- Score

25. Whom do you really need or want to serve?
<--- Score

26. Are there regulatory / compliance issues?
<--- Score

27. How can auditing be a preventative security measure?
<--- Score

28. How much are sponsors, customers, partners, stakeholders involved in Improve Operation? In other words, what are the risks, if Improve Operation does not deliver successfully?
<--- Score

29. What are the minority interests and what amount of minority interests can be recognized?
<--- Score

30. What are the stakeholder objectives to be achieved with Improve Operation?
<--- Score

31. Which needs are not included or involved?
<--- Score

32. As a sponsor, customer or management, how important is it to meet goals, objectives?
<--- Score

33. What is the problem or issue?
<--- Score

34. How are the Improve Operation's objectives aligned to the group's overall stakeholder strategy?
<--- Score

35. Are there recognized Improve Operation problems?
<--- Score

36. Who else hopes to benefit from it?
<--- Score

37. What situation(s) led to this Improve Operation Self Assessment?
<--- Score

38. What should be considered when identifying available resources, constraints, and deadlines?
<--- Score

39. To what extent would your organization benefit from being recognized as a award recipient?
<--- Score

40. Does your organization need more Improve Operation education?
<--- Score

41. What activities does the governance board need to consider?
<--- Score

42. What are the timeframes required to resolve each of the issues/problems?
<--- Score

43. How do you recognize an objection?
<--- Score

44. Did you miss any major Improve Operation issues?
<--- Score

45. Is it clear when you think of the day ahead of you what activities and tasks you need to complete?
<--- Score

46. Are problem definition and motivation clearly presented?
<--- Score

47. What information do users need?
<--- Score

48. Are losses recognized in a timely manner?
<--- Score

49. What Improve Operation problem should be solved?
<--- Score

50. What needs to be done?
<--- Score

51. What else needs to be measured?
<--- Score

52. Are there any specific expectations or concerns about the Improve Operation team, Improve Operation itself?
<--- Score

53. Are there any revenue recognition issues?
<--- Score

54. What is the smallest subset of the problem you can usefully solve?
<--- Score

55. What is the extent or complexity of the Improve Operation problem?
<--- Score

56. Will it solve real problems?
<--- Score

57. What prevents you from making the changes you know will make you a more effective Improve Operation leader?
<--- Score

58. Who needs to know about Improve Operation?
<--- Score

59. What are the Improve Operation resources needed?
<--- Score

60. Does the problem have ethical dimensions?
<--- Score

61. Do you have/need 24-hour access to key personnel?
<--- Score

62. Have you identified your Improve Operation key performance indicators?
<--- Score

63. How are you going to measure success?
<--- Score

64. What is the problem and/or vulnerability?
<--- Score

65. Do you recognize Improve Operation achievements?
<--- Score

66. What extra resources will you need?
<--- Score

67. Think about the people you identified for your Improve Operation project and the project responsibilities you would assign to them, what kind of training do you think they would need to perform these responsibilities effectively?
<--- Score

68. Which information does the Improve Operation business case need to include?
<--- Score

69. What problems are you facing and how do you consider Improve Operation will circumvent those obstacles?

<--- Score

70. Does Improve Operation create potential expectations in other areas that need to be recognized and considered?
<--- Score

71. Why is this needed?
<--- Score

72. Will a response program recognize when a crisis occurs and provide some level of response?
<--- Score

73. Is the need for organizational change recognized?
<--- Score

74. Why the need?
<--- Score

75. Who needs what information?
<--- Score

76. What training and capacity building actions are needed to implement proposed reforms?
<--- Score

77. Are you dealing with any of the same issues today as yesterday? What can you do about this?
<--- Score

78. What needs to stay?
<--- Score

79. Who needs to know?
<--- Score

80. What tools and technologies are needed for a custom Improve Operation project?
<--- Score

81. Can management personnel recognize the monetary benefit of Improve Operation?
<--- Score

82. Would you recognize a threat from the inside?
<--- Score

83. How does it fit into your organizational needs and tasks?
<--- Score

84. Who needs budgets?
<--- Score

85. How are training requirements identified?
<--- Score

86. Do you need to avoid or amend any Improve Operation activities?
<--- Score

87. What do employees need in the short term?
<--- Score

88. Is the quality assurance team identified?
<--- Score

89. How do you take a forward-looking perspective in identifying Improve Operation research related to market response and models?
<--- Score

90. How do you recognize an Improve Operation objection?
<--- Score

91. How many trainings, in total, are needed?
<--- Score

92. What do you need to start doing?
<--- Score

93. What does Improve Operation success mean to the stakeholders?
<--- Score

94. Who defines the rules in relation to any given issue?
<--- Score

95. Do you need different information or graphics?
<--- Score

96. Who should resolve the Improve Operation issues?
<--- Score

97. For your Improve Operation project, identify and describe the business environment, is there more than one layer to the business environment?
<--- Score

98. To what extent does each concerned units management team recognize Improve Operation as an effective investment?
<--- Score

99. Are there Improve Operation problems defined?

<--- Score

Add up total points for this section:
_ _ _ _ _ = Total points for this section

Divided by: _ _ _ _ _ _ (number of
statements answered) = _ _ _ _ _ _
Average score for this section

Transfer your score to the Improve
Operation Index at the beginning of the
Self-Assessment.

CRITERION #2: DEFINE:

INTENT: Formulate the stakeholder problem. Define the problem, needs and objectives.

In my belief, the answer to this question is clearly defined:

5 Strongly Agree

4 Agree

3 Neutral

2 Disagree

1 Strongly Disagree

1. If substitutes have been appointed, have they been briefed on the Improve Operation goals and received regular communications as to the progress to date?
<--- Score

2. What gets examined?
<--- Score

3. What knowledge or experience is required?

<--- Score

4. Who are the Improve Operation improvement team members, including Management Leads and Coaches?
<--- Score

5. How do you hand over Improve Operation context?
<--- Score

6. Has the Improve Operation work been fairly and/ or equitably divided and delegated among team members who are qualified and capable to perform the work? Has everyone contributed?
<--- Score

7. Is there a Improve Operation management charter, including stakeholder case, problem and goal statements, scope, milestones, roles and responsibilities, communication plan?
<--- Score

8. What customer feedback methods were used to solicit their input?
<--- Score

9. What are the compelling stakeholder reasons for embarking on Improve Operation?
<--- Score

10. What are the requirements for audit information?
<--- Score

11. What sources do you use to gather information for a Improve Operation study?
<--- Score

12. Will team members regularly document their Improve Operation work?
<--- Score

13. What are the core elements of the Improve Operation business case?
<--- Score

14. Is the scope of Improve Operation defined?
<--- Score

15. What are the Improve Operation tasks and definitions?
<--- Score

16. Is there a critical path to deliver Improve Operation results?
<--- Score

17. Do you have a Improve Operation success story or case study ready to tell and share?
<--- Score

18. What is the scope of Improve Operation?
<--- Score

19. Has everyone on the team, including the team leaders, been properly trained?
<--- Score

20. Is Improve Operation linked to key stakeholder goals and objectives?
<--- Score

21. How did the Improve Operation manager receive

input to the development of a Improve Operation improvement plan and the estimated completion dates/times of each activity?
<--- Score

22. Are accountability and ownership for Improve Operation clearly defined?
<--- Score

23. Who is gathering Improve Operation information?
<--- Score

24. Has/have the customer(s) been identified?
<--- Score

25. How do you build the right business case?
<--- Score

26. What are the boundaries of the scope? What is in bounds and what is not? What is the start point? What is the stop point?
<--- Score

27. Who is gathering information?
<--- Score

28. When are meeting minutes sent out? Who is on the distribution list?
<--- Score

29. When is/was the Improve Operation start date?
<--- Score

30. How do you keep key subject matter experts in the loop?
<--- Score

31. How is the team tracking and documenting its work?
<--- Score

32. In what way can you redefine the criteria of choice clients have in your category in your favor?
<--- Score

33. What is out of scope?
<--- Score

34. Is the team equipped with available and reliable resources?
<--- Score

35. What baselines are required to be defined and managed?
<--- Score

36. Is the improvement team aware of the different versions of a process: what they think it is vs. what it actually is vs. what it should be vs. what it could be?
<--- Score

37. What is in scope?
<--- Score

38. Are audit criteria, scope, frequency and methods defined?
<--- Score

39. Is the current 'as is' process being followed? If not, what are the discrepancies?
<--- Score

40. Is there a clear Improve Operation case definition?
<--- Score

41. Is there a completed, verified, and validated high-level 'as is' (not 'should be' or 'could be') stakeholder process map?
<--- Score

42. How do you manage unclear Improve Operation requirements?
<--- Score

43. What are the tasks and definitions?
<--- Score

44. Is there any additional Improve Operation definition of success?
<--- Score

45. What intelligence can you gather?
<--- Score

46. What are (control) requirements for Improve Operation Information?
<--- Score

47. What specifically is the problem? Where does it occur? When does it occur? What is its extent?
<--- Score

48. Has a high-level 'as is' process map been completed, verified and validated?
<--- Score

49. How are consistent Improve Operation definitions important?

<--- Score

50. How will the Improve Operation team and the group measure complete success of Improve Operation?
<--- Score

51. What is the worst case scenario?
<--- Score

52. What critical content must be communicated – who, what, when, where, and how?
<--- Score

53. Have the customer needs been translated into specific, measurable requirements? How?
<--- Score

54. How do you think the partners involved in Improve Operation would have defined success?
<--- Score

55. How do you manage changes in Improve Operation requirements?
<--- Score

56. Have all basic functions of Improve Operation been defined?
<--- Score

57. Are there any constraints known that bear on the ability to perform Improve Operation work? How is the team addressing them?
<--- Score

58. Are task requirements clearly defined?

<--- Score

59. Why are you doing Improve Operation and what is the scope?
<--- Score

60. What was the context?
<--- Score

61. Is it clearly defined in and to your organization what you do?
<--- Score

62. Scope of sensitive information?
<--- Score

63. What is the definition of Improve Operation excellence?
<--- Score

64. How do you manage scope?
<--- Score

65. Do you have organizational privacy requirements?
<--- Score

66. What is the context?
<--- Score

67. Are approval levels defined for contracts and supplements to contracts?
<--- Score

68. Are different versions of process maps needed to account for the different types of inputs?
<--- Score

69. Has a team charter been developed and communicated?
<--- Score

70. Will team members perform Improve Operation work when assigned and in a timely fashion?
<--- Score

71. Are required metrics defined, what are they?
<--- Score

72. Do the problem and goal statements meet the SMART criteria (specific, measurable, attainable, relevant, and time-bound)?
<--- Score

73. Are the Improve Operation requirements testable?
<--- Score

74. Where can you gather more information?
<--- Score

75. What constraints exist that might impact the team?
<--- Score

76. How do you catch Improve Operation definition inconsistencies?
<--- Score

77. What scope to assess?
<--- Score

78. Is the team adequately staffed with the desired cross-functionality? If not, what additional resources

are available to the team?
<--- Score

79. Is special Improve Operation user knowledge required?
<--- Score

80. When is the estimated completion date?
<--- Score

81. What is a worst-case scenario for losses?
<--- Score

82. What key stakeholder process output measure(s) does Improve Operation leverage and how?
<--- Score

83. Are customer(s) identified and segmented according to their different needs and requirements?
<--- Score

84. How do you gather the stories?
<--- Score

85. Does the team have regular meetings?
<--- Score

86. How have you defined all Improve Operation requirements first?
<--- Score

87. What would be the goal or target for a Improve Operation's improvement team?
<--- Score

88. How would you define the culture at your

organization, how susceptible is it to Improve Operation changes?
<--- Score

89. Is there a completed SIPOC representation, describing the Suppliers, Inputs, Process, Outputs, and Customers?
<--- Score

90. What happens if Improve Operation's scope changes?
<--- Score

91. What scope do you want your strategy to cover?
<--- Score

92. Do you all define Improve Operation in the same way?
<--- Score

93. What are the dynamics of the communication plan?
<--- Score

94. Is the Improve Operation scope complete and appropriately sized?
<--- Score

95. How was the 'as is' process map developed, reviewed, verified and validated?
<--- Score

96. What defines best in class?
<--- Score

97. Are resources adequate for the scope?

<--- Score

98. Has a project plan, Gantt chart, or similar been developed/completed?
<--- Score

99. What is out-of-scope initially?
<--- Score

100. Is the work to date meeting requirements?
<--- Score

101. What Improve Operation requirements should be gathered?
<--- Score

102. What information do you gather?
<--- Score

103. Does the scope remain the same?
<--- Score

104. Are there different segments of customers?
<--- Score

105. Is full participation by members in regularly held team meetings guaranteed?
<--- Score

106. Is the Improve Operation scope manageable?
<--- Score

107. Who defines (or who defined) the rules and roles?
<--- Score

108. How often are the team meetings?

<--- Score

109. What Improve Operation services do you require?
<--- Score

110. Has the improvement team collected the 'voice of the customer' (obtained feedback – qualitative and quantitative)?
<--- Score

111. Is there regularly 100% attendance at the team meetings? If not, have appointed substitutes attended to preserve cross-functionality and full representation?
<--- Score

112. What is in the scope and what is not in scope?
<--- Score

113. Has a Improve Operation requirement not been met?
<--- Score

114. Have specific policy objectives been defined?
<--- Score

115. What are the Improve Operation use cases?
<--- Score

116. Has anyone else (internal or external to the group) attempted to solve this problem or a similar one before? If so, what knowledge can be leveraged from these previous efforts?
<--- Score

117. Has the direction changed at all during the

course of Improve Operation? If so, when did it change and why?
<--- Score

118. What system do you use for gathering Improve Operation information?
<--- Score

119. How do you gather requirements?
<--- Score

120. Are all requirements met?
<--- Score

121. Is scope creep really all bad news?
<--- Score

122. What is the definition of success?
<--- Score

123. Is Improve Operation currently on schedule according to the plan?
<--- Score

124. Who approved the Improve Operation scope?
<--- Score

125. Are the Improve Operation requirements complete?
<--- Score

126. Is Improve Operation required?
<--- Score

127. What are the record-keeping requirements of Improve Operation activities?

<--- Score

128. Is data collected and displayed to better understand customer(s) critical needs and requirements.
<--- Score

129. The political context: who holds power?
<--- Score

130. How will variation in the actual durations of each activity be dealt with to ensure that the expected Improve Operation results are met?
<--- Score

131. Will a Improve Operation production readiness review be required?
<--- Score

132. What are the Roles and Responsibilities for each team member and its leadership? Where is this documented?
<--- Score

133. Are roles and responsibilities formally defined?
<--- Score

134. How does the Improve Operation manager ensure against scope creep?
<--- Score

135. What are the rough order estimates on cost savings/opportunities that Improve Operation brings?
<--- Score

136. What information should you gather?

<--- Score

Add up total points for this section:
_ _ _ _ _ = Total points for this section

Divided by: _ _ _ _ _ _ (number of
statements answered) = _ _ _ _ _ _
Average score for this section

Transfer your score to the Improve
Operation Index at the beginning of the
Self-Assessment.

CRITERION #3: MEASURE:

INTENT: Gather the correct data. Measure the current performance and evolution of the situation.

In my belief, the answer to this question is clearly defined:

5 Strongly Agree

4 Agree

3 Neutral

2 Disagree

1 Strongly Disagree

1. What do people want to verify?
<--- Score

2. Do you aggressively reward and promote the people who have the biggest impact on creating excellent Improve Operation services/products?
<--- Score

3. How will your organization measure success?

<--- Score

4. What is an unallowable cost?
<--- Score

5. What is the Improve Operation business impact?
<--- Score

6. Which costs should be taken into account?
<--- Score

7. Is there an opportunity to verify requirements?
<--- Score

8. How do you verify the Improve Operation requirements quality?
<--- Score

9. Where can you go to verify the info?
<--- Score

10. What happens if cost savings do not materialize?
<--- Score

11. How will costs be allocated?
<--- Score

12. What are your key Improve Operation organizational performance measures, including key short and longer-term financial measures?
<--- Score

13. Where is the cost?
<--- Score

14. What details are required of the Improve

Operation cost structure?
<--- Score

15. When should you bother with diagrams?
<--- Score

16. How do you measure variability?
<--- Score

17. What are the costs of delaying Improve Operation action?
<--- Score

18. What methods are feasible and acceptable to estimate the impact of reforms?
<--- Score

19. What are the costs?
<--- Score

20. Are supply costs steady or fluctuating?
<--- Score

21. Do the benefits outweigh the costs?
<--- Score

22. How much does it cost?
<--- Score

23. What are your customers expectations and measures?
<--- Score

24. When are costs are incurred?
<--- Score

25. What causes mismanagement?
<--- Score

26. How do you verify your resources?
<--- Score

27. How are costs allocated?
<--- Score

28. What is the cost of rework?
<--- Score

29. Are there competing Improve Operation priorities?
<--- Score

30. Are Improve Operation vulnerabilities categorized and prioritized?
<--- Score

31. What causes investor action?
<--- Score

32. What does verifying compliance entail?
<--- Score

33. What is your decision requirements diagram?
<--- Score

34. How frequently do you verify your Improve Operation strategy?
<--- Score

35. What does your operating model cost?
<--- Score

36. How do you control the overall costs of your work

processes?
<--- Score

37. Does the Improve Operation task fit the client's priorities?
<--- Score

38. Why do you expend time and effort to implement measurement, for whom?
<--- Score

39. How do you verify Improve Operation completeness and accuracy?
<--- Score

40. How do you aggregate measures across priorities?
<--- Score

41. What harm might be caused?
<--- Score

42. Why do the measurements/indicators matter?
<--- Score

43. How is performance measured?
<--- Score

44. What do you measure and why?
<--- Score

45. Are you aware of what could cause a problem?
<--- Score

46. How do your measurements capture actionable Improve Operation information for use in exceeding your customers expectations and securing your

customers engagement?
<--- Score

47. How do you measure lifecycle phases?
<--- Score

48. Are there measurements based on task performance?
<--- Score

49. What potential environmental factors impact the Improve Operation effort?
<--- Score

50. What are the uncertainties surrounding estimates of impact?
<--- Score

51. What measurements are being captured?
<--- Score

52. How is the value delivered by Improve Operation being measured?
<--- Score

53. How will you measure success?
<--- Score

54. Have design-to-cost goals been established?
<--- Score

55. What is your Improve Operation quality cost segregation study?
<--- Score

56. Who should receive measurement reports?

<--- Score

57. Have you made assumptions about the shape of the future, particularly its impact on your customers and competitors?
<--- Score

58. Are you able to realize any cost savings?
<--- Score

59. What is the total fixed cost?
<--- Score

60. Do you effectively measure and reward individual and team performance?
<--- Score

61. What users will be impacted?
<--- Score

62. How will you measure your Improve Operation effectiveness?
<--- Score

63. What is the root cause(s) of the problem?
<--- Score

64. How do you prevent mis-estimating cost?
<--- Score

65. What could cause delays in the schedule?
<--- Score

66. Are indirect costs charged to the Improve Operation program?
<--- Score

67. Which measures and indicators matter?
<--- Score

68. How do you verify performance?
<--- Score

69. What are the costs of reform?
<--- Score

70. When a disaster occurs, who gets priority?
<--- Score

71. Are actual costs in line with budgeted costs?
<--- Score

72. Does management have the right priorities among projects?
<--- Score

73. What are the types and number of measures to use?
<--- Score

74. Do you have a flow diagram of what happens?
<--- Score

75. Are there any easy-to-implement alternatives to Improve Operation? Sometimes other solutions are available that do not require the cost implications of a full-blown project?
<--- Score

76. What are the estimated costs of proposed changes?
<--- Score

77. How sensitive must the Improve Operation strategy be to cost?
<--- Score

78. What causes innovation to fail or succeed in your organization?
<--- Score

79. Are the units of measure consistent?
<--- Score

80. How long to keep data and how to manage retention costs?
<--- Score

81. Do you have any cost Improve Operation limitation requirements?
<--- Score

82. How can a Improve Operation test verify your ideas or assumptions?
<--- Score

83. How can you manage cost down?
<--- Score

84. What are the current costs of the Improve Operation process?
<--- Score

85. Is the solution cost-effective?
<--- Score

86. Did you tackle the cause or the symptom?
<--- Score

87. What does losing customers cost your organization?
<--- Score

88. Are missed Improve Operation opportunities costing your organization money?
<--- Score

89. How do you measure success?
<--- Score

90. Is the cost worth the Improve Operation effort ?
<--- Score

91. How are measurements made?
<--- Score

92. What evidence is there and what is measured?
<--- Score

93. What tests verify requirements?
<--- Score

94. How will effects be measured?
<--- Score

95. How are you verifying it?
<--- Score

96. What is measured? Why?
<--- Score

97. What are hidden Improve Operation quality costs?
<--- Score

98. What are the strategic priorities for this year?
<--- Score

99. Where is it measured?
<--- Score

100. How frequently do you track Improve Operation measures?
<--- Score

101. Will Improve Operation have an impact on current business continuity, disaster recovery processes and/or infrastructure?
<--- Score

102. Which Improve Operation impacts are significant?
<--- Score

103. How to cause the change?
<--- Score

104. Do you have an issue in getting priority?
<--- Score

105. What would it cost to replace your technology?
<--- Score

106. At what cost?
<--- Score

107. Do you verify that corrective actions were taken?
<--- Score

108. Are you taking your company in the direction of better and revenue or cheaper and cost?

<--- Score

109. What are allowable costs?
<--- Score

110. What are your primary costs, revenues, assets?
<--- Score

111. What does a Test Case verify?
<--- Score

112. Was a business case (cost/benefit) developed?
<--- Score

113. How do you verify and develop ideas and innovations?
<--- Score

114. The approach of traditional Improve Operation works for detail complexity but is focused on a systematic approach rather than an understanding of the nature of systems themselves, what approach will permit your organization to deal with the kind of unpredictable emergent behaviors that dynamic complexity can introduce?
<--- Score

115. How do you measure efficient delivery of Improve Operation services?
<--- Score

116. Is it possible to estimate the impact of unanticipated complexity such as wrong or failed assumptions, feedback, etcetera on proposed reforms?
<--- Score

117. Among the Improve Operation product and service cost to be estimated, which is considered hardest to estimate?
<--- Score

118. What would be a real cause for concern?
<--- Score

119. What measurements are possible, practicable and meaningful?
<--- Score

120. What are the Improve Operation key cost drivers?
<--- Score

121. How will success or failure be measured?
<--- Score

122. Why a Improve Operation focus?
<--- Score

123. How can you measure the performance?
<--- Score

124. What causes extra work or rework?
<--- Score

125. Have you included everything in your Improve Operation cost models?
<--- Score

126. How is progress measured?
<--- Score

127. What are you verifying?

<--- Score

128. What are your operating costs?
<--- Score

129. Who pays the cost?
<--- Score

130. Are the measurements objective?
<--- Score

131. Has a cost center been established?
<--- Score

132. How do you verify and validate the Improve
Operation data?
<--- Score

133. Who is involved in verifying compliance?
<--- Score

134. What relevant entities could be measured?
<--- Score

135. How do you verify the authenticity of the data
and information used?
<--- Score

136. How will measures be used to manage and
adapt?
<--- Score

137. Does a Improve Operation quantification method
exist?
<--- Score

138. What is the cause of any Improve Operation gaps?
<--- Score

139. How can you reduce the costs of obtaining inputs?
<--- Score

140. How do you verify if Improve Operation is built right?
<--- Score

141. How can you reduce costs?
<--- Score

142. What are the costs and benefits?
<--- Score

Add up total points for this section:
_ _ _ _ _ = Total points for this section

Divided by: _ _ _ _ _ _ (number of statements answered) = _ _ _ _ _ _
Average score for this section

Transfer your score to the Improve Operation Index at the beginning of the Self-Assessment.

CRITERION #4: ANALYZE:

INTENT: Analyze causes, assumptions and hypotheses.

In my belief, the answer to this question is clearly defined:

5 Strongly Agree

4 Agree

3 Neutral

2 Disagree

1 Strongly Disagree

1. How is data used for program management and improvement?
<--- Score

2. Who is involved in the management review process?
<--- Score

3. What qualifications do Improve Operation leaders need?

<--- Score

4. Where can you get qualified talent today?
<--- Score

5. How do you measure the operational performance of your key work systems and processes, including productivity, cycle time, and other appropriate measures of process effectiveness, efficiency, and innovation?
<--- Score

6. How difficult is it to qualify what Improve Operation ROI is?
<--- Score

7. What is the complexity of the output produced?
<--- Score

8. Are all staff in core Improve Operation subjects Highly Qualified?
<--- Score

9. What is the cost of poor quality as supported by the team's analysis?
<--- Score

10. What are the personnel training and qualifications required?
<--- Score

11. Who gets your output?
<--- Score

12. What other jobs or tasks affect the performance of the steps in the Improve Operation process?

<--- Score

13. Do several people in different organizational units assist with the Improve Operation process?
<--- Score

14. What are your key performance measures or indicators and in-process measures for the control and improvement of your Improve Operation processes?
<--- Score

15. What, related to, Improve Operation processes does your organization outsource?
<--- Score

16. How do mission and objectives affect the Improve Operation processes of your organization?
<--- Score

17. Identify an operational issue in your organization, for example, could a particular task be done more quickly or more efficiently by Improve Operation?
<--- Score

18. Is the Improve Operation process severely broken such that a re-design is necessary?
<--- Score

19. What are your best practices for minimizing Improve Operation project risk, while demonstrating incremental value and quick wins throughout the Improve Operation project lifecycle?
<--- Score

20. How will the change process be managed?

<--- Score

21. Is the performance gap determined?
<--- Score

22. What do you need to qualify?
<--- Score

23. What process should you select for improvement?
<--- Score

24. What systems/processes must you excel at?
<--- Score

25. Were any designed experiments used to generate additional insight into the data analysis?
<--- Score

26. Think about the functions involved in your Improve Operation project, what processes flow from these functions?
<--- Score

27. What methods do you use to gather Improve Operation data?
<--- Score

28. What internal processes need improvement?
<--- Score

29. What are your current levels and trends in key Improve Operation measures or indicators of product and process performance that are important to and directly serve your customers?
<--- Score

30. What training and qualifications will you need?
<--- Score

31. Was a cause-and-effect diagram used to explore the different types of causes (or sources of variation)?
<--- Score

32. What are the necessary qualifications?
<--- Score

33. How much data can be collected in the given timeframe?
<--- Score

34. How will corresponding data be collected?
<--- Score

35. What are your Improve Operation processes?
<--- Score

36. Is there a strict change management process?
<--- Score

37. What are the processes for audit reporting and management?
<--- Score

38. Has an output goal been set?
<--- Score

39. Is data and process analysis, root cause analysis and quantifying the gap/opportunity in place?
<--- Score

40. What qualifications are needed?
<--- Score

41. How often will data be collected for measures?
<--- Score

42. Are all team members qualified for all tasks?
<--- Score

43. Do your contracts/agreements contain data security obligations?
<--- Score

44. What is the oversight process?
<--- Score

45. Should you invest in industry-recognized qualifications?
<--- Score

46. What were the financial benefits resulting from any 'ground fruit or low-hanging fruit' (quick fixes)?
<--- Score

47. Do your leaders quickly bounce back from setbacks?
<--- Score

48. Are your outputs consistent?
<--- Score

49. Do staff qualifications match your project?
<--- Score

50. What qualifications are necessary?
<--- Score

51. Think about some of the processes you undertake

within your organization, which do you own?
<--- Score

52. Is the required Improve Operation data gathered?
<--- Score

53. Who is involved with workflow mapping?
<--- Score

54. How do you use Improve Operation data and information to support organizational decision making and innovation?
<--- Score

55. How are outputs preserved and protected?
<--- Score

56. What are the best opportunities for value improvement?
<--- Score

57. Is the final output clearly identified?
<--- Score

58. When should a process be art not science?
<--- Score

59. Do you understand your management processes today?
<--- Score

60. What is your organizations system for selecting qualified vendors?
<--- Score

61. What other organizational variables, such as

reward systems or communication systems, affect the performance of this Improve Operation process?
<--- Score

62. Is there an established change management process?
<--- Score

63. What quality tools were used to get through the analyze phase?
<--- Score

64. What are your current levels and trends in key measures or indicators of Improve Operation product and process performance that are important to and directly serve your customers? How do these results compare with the performance of your competitors and other organizations with similar offerings?
<--- Score

65. What does the data say about the performance of the stakeholder process?
<--- Score

66. Have the problem and goal statements been updated to reflect the additional knowledge gained from the analyze phase?
<--- Score

67. How do you define collaboration and team output?
<--- Score

68. What did the team gain from developing a sub-process map?
<--- Score

69. Do quality systems drive continuous improvement?
<--- Score

70. What are the Improve Operation design outputs?
<--- Score

71. What qualifications and skills do you need?
<--- Score

72. What successful thing are you doing today that may be blinding you to new growth opportunities?
<--- Score

73. Who qualifies to gain access to data?
<--- Score

74. What output to create?
<--- Score

75. How does the organization define, manage, and improve its Improve Operation processes?
<--- Score

76. What Improve Operation metrics are outputs of the process?
<--- Score

77. What data is gathered?
<--- Score

78. Who owns what data?
<--- Score

79. Is the suppliers process defined and controlled?

<--- Score

80. What will drive Improve Operation change?
<--- Score

81. What Improve Operation data will be collected?
<--- Score

82. Is pre-qualification of suppliers carried out?
<--- Score

83. How do you implement and manage your work processes to ensure that they meet design requirements?
<--- Score

84. What are evaluation criteria for the output?
<--- Score

85. Who will gather what data?
<--- Score

86. What tools were used to narrow the list of possible causes?
<--- Score

87. What Improve Operation data should be collected?
<--- Score

88. What are the disruptive Improve Operation technologies that enable your organization to radically change your business processes?
<--- Score

89. Can you add value to the current Improve

Operation decision-making process (largely qualitative) by incorporating uncertainty modeling (more quantitative)?
<--- Score

90. Have any additional benefits been identified that will result from closing all or most of the gaps?
<--- Score

91. What is the Improve Operation Driver?
<--- Score

92. What conclusions were drawn from the team's data collection and analysis? How did the team reach these conclusions?
<--- Score

93. How do you ensure that the Improve Operation opportunity is realistic?
<--- Score

94. Where is Improve Operation data gathered?
<--- Score

95. What tools were used to generate the list of possible causes?
<--- Score

96. What resources go in to get the desired output?
<--- Score

97. Were there any improvement opportunities identified from the process analysis?
<--- Score

98. How will the Improve Operation data be captured?

<--- Score

99. How do your work systems and key work processes relate to and capitalize on your core competencies?
<--- Score

100. How is the Improve Operation Value Stream Mapping managed?
<--- Score

101. How many input/output points does it require?
<--- Score

102. No matter what your mission, a more digital approach to organizational processes will improve operations in dramatic and easily measured ways. What matters most to your organization?
<--- Score

103. What are your outputs?
<--- Score

104. What Improve Operation data should be managed?
<--- Score

105. Are you missing Improve Operation opportunities?
<--- Score

106. What is the Value Stream Mapping?
<--- Score

107. Which Improve Operation data should be retained?

<--- Score

108. A compounding model resolution with available relevant data can often provide insight towards a solution methodology; which Improve Operation models, tools and techniques are necessary?
<--- Score

109. How is the way you as the leader think and process information affecting your organizational culture?
<--- Score

110. What Improve Operation data do you gather or use now?
<--- Score

111. Has data output been validated?
<--- Score

112. What were the crucial 'moments of truth' on the process map?
<--- Score

113. How can risk management be tied procedurally to process elements?
<--- Score

114. How is the data gathered?
<--- Score

115. Do your employees have the opportunity to do what they do best everyday?
<--- Score

116. Are Improve Operation changes recognized early

enough to be approved through the regular process?
<--- Score

117. What are the Improve Operation business drivers?
<--- Score

118. What controls do you have in place to protect data?
<--- Score

119. How do you promote understanding that opportunity for improvement is not criticism of the status quo, or the people who created the status quo?
<--- Score

120. How do you identify specific Improve Operation investment opportunities and emerging trends?
<--- Score

121. Is there any way to speed up the process?
<--- Score

122. Were Pareto charts (or similar) used to portray the 'heavy hitters' (or key sources of variation)?
<--- Score

123. What data do you need to collect?
<--- Score

124. How will the data be checked for quality?
<--- Score

125. How has the Improve Operation data been gathered?
<--- Score

126. How was the detailed process map generated, verified, and validated?
<--- Score

127. What qualifies as competition?
<--- Score

128. Is the gap/opportunity displayed and communicated in financial terms?
<--- Score

129. How is Improve Operation data gathered?
<--- Score

130. What are the revised rough estimates of the financial savings/opportunity for Improve Operation improvements?
<--- Score

131. What is the output?
<--- Score

132. Record-keeping requirements flow from the records needed as inputs, outputs, controls and for transformation of a Improve Operation process, are the records needed as inputs to the Improve Operation process available?
<--- Score

133. Who will facilitate the team and process?
<--- Score

134. What information qualified as important?
<--- Score

135. What kind of crime could a potential new hire have committed that would not only not disqualify him/her from being hired by your organization, but would actually indicate that he/she might be a particularly good fit?
<--- Score

136. What types of data do your Improve Operation indicators require?
<--- Score

137. Was a detailed process map created to amplify critical steps of the 'as is' stakeholder process?
<--- Score

Add up total points for this section:
_ _ _ _ _ = Total points for this section

Divided by: _ _ _ _ _ _ (number of statements answered) = _ _ _ _ _ _ Average score for this section

Transfer your score to the Improve Operation Index at the beginning of the Self-Assessment.

CRITERION #5: IMPROVE:

INTENT: Develop a practical solution. Innovate, establish and test the solution and to measure the results.

In my belief, the answer to this question is clearly defined:

5 Strongly Agree

4 Agree

3 Neutral

2 Disagree

1 Strongly Disagree

1. Who are the Improve Operation decision makers?
<--- Score

2. Does the goal represent a desired result that can be measured?
<--- Score

3. How do you measure improved Improve Operation service perception, and satisfaction?

<--- Score

4. What tools were most useful during the improve phase?
<--- Score

5. Is there any other Improve Operation solution?
<--- Score

6. Is any Improve Operation documentation required?
<--- Score

7. Where do the Improve Operation decisions reside?
<--- Score

8. Who will be responsible for making the decisions to include or exclude requested changes once Improve Operation is underway?
<--- Score

9. Risk Identification: What are the possible risk events your organization faces in relation to Improve Operation?
<--- Score

10. How significant is the improvement in the eyes of the end user?
<--- Score

11. Would you develop a Improve Operation Communication Strategy?
<--- Score

12. What risks do you need to manage?
<--- Score

13. How will you know that you have improved?
<--- Score

14. Is the measure of success for Improve Operation understandable to a variety of people?
<--- Score

15. What tools were used to evaluate the potential solutions?
<--- Score

16. What current systems have to be understood and/ or changed?
<--- Score

17. What are your current levels and trends in key measures or indicators of workforce and leader development?
<--- Score

18. How is continuous improvement applied to risk management?
<--- Score

19. What resources are required for the improvement efforts?
<--- Score

20. Is the scope clearly documented?
<--- Score

21. How do you manage and improve your Improve Operation work systems to deliver customer value and achieve organizational success and sustainability?
<--- Score

22. How can you improve Improve Operation?
<--- Score

23. How is knowledge sharing about risk management improved?
<--- Score

24. What assumptions are made about the solution and approach?
<--- Score

25. Actionable - can you take action with your metrics to improve operations?
<--- Score

26. Who do you report Improve Operation results to?
<--- Score

27. How do you measure progress and evaluate training effectiveness?
<--- Score

28. Are the key business and technology risks being managed?
<--- Score

29. How does your organization evaluate strategic Improve Operation success?
<--- Score

30. If you could go back in time five years, what decision would you make differently? What is your best guess as to what decision you're making today you might regret five years from now?
<--- Score

31. Who are the key stakeholders for the Improve Operation evaluation?
<--- Score

32. How scalable is your Improve Operation solution?
<--- Score

33. What alternative responses are available to manage risk?
<--- Score

34. What should a proof of concept or pilot accomplish?
<--- Score

35. How do the Improve Operation results compare with the performance of your competitors and other organizations with similar offerings?
<--- Score

36. To which degree do you think it could help improve operational culture?
<--- Score

37. For decision problems, how do you develop a decision statement?
<--- Score

38. Who are the Improve Operation decision-makers?
<--- Score

39. Are risk management tasks balanced centrally and locally?
<--- Score

40. How do you improve Improve Operation service

perception, and satisfaction?
<--- Score

41. Who makes the Improve Operation decisions in your organization?
<--- Score

42. Can you integrate quality management and risk management?
<--- Score

43. Is there a high likelihood that any recommendations will achieve their intended results?
<--- Score

44. At what point will vulnerability assessments be performed once Improve Operation is put into production (e.g., ongoing Risk Management after implementation)?
<--- Score

45. How do you keep improving Improve Operation?
<--- Score

46. Can the solution be designed and implemented within an acceptable time period?
<--- Score

47. How can 3D scanning be applied to improve operations and maintenance of your existing assets?
<--- Score

48. What is the risk?
<--- Score

49. How will you know that a change is an improvement?
<--- Score

50. What are the affordable Improve Operation risks?
<--- Score

51. How are policy decisions made and where?
<--- Score

52. How do you deal with Improve Operation risk?
<--- Score

53. What is the magnitude of the improvements?
<--- Score

54. What can you do to improve?
<--- Score

55. Are procedures documented for managing Improve Operation risks?
<--- Score

56. How is Business Intelligence used in your operational excellence initiative to improve operational efficiency?
<--- Score

57. Where do you need Improve Operation improvement?
<--- Score

58. Who will be using the results of the measurement activities?
<--- Score

59. Are risk triggers captured?
<--- Score

60. Do you have the optimal project management team structure?
<--- Score

61. What went well, what should change, what can improve?
<--- Score

62. Does a good decision guarantee a good outcome?
<--- Score

63. Who controls the risk?
<--- Score

64. In the past few months, what is the smallest change you have made that has had the biggest positive result? What was it about that small change that produced the large return?
<--- Score

65. Who controls key decisions that will be made?
<--- Score

66. Who should make the Improve Operation decisions?
<--- Score

67. How does your organization use performance results to improve operations (using each method)?
<--- Score

68. How do you define the solutions' scope?

<--- Score

69. Can you identify any significant risks or exposures to Improve Operation third- parties (vendors, service providers, alliance partners etc) that concern you?
<--- Score

70. What tools were used to tap into the creativity and encourage 'outside the box' thinking?
<--- Score

71. Who manages Improve Operation risk?
<--- Score

72. How do you improve your likelihood of success ?
<--- Score

73. Are the most efficient solutions problem-specific?
<--- Score

74. What were the underlying assumptions on the cost-benefit analysis?
<--- Score

75. How will you know when its improved?
<--- Score

76. Improve Operation risk decisions: whose call Is It?
<--- Score

77. How will you recognize and celebrate results?
<--- Score

78. What are the Improve Operation security risks?
<--- Score

79. Who will be responsible for documenting the Improve Operation requirements in detail?
<--- Score

80. What to do with the results or outcomes of measurements?
<--- Score

81. Which of the recognised risks out of all risks can be most likely transferred?
<--- Score

82. What were the criteria for evaluating a Improve Operation pilot?
<--- Score

83. What needs improvement? Why?
<--- Score

84. What tools do you use once you have decided on a Improve Operation strategy and more importantly how do you choose?
<--- Score

85. How risky is your organization?
<--- Score

86. What do you want to improve?
<--- Score

87. Is the solution technically practical?
<--- Score

88. What lessons, if any, from a pilot were incorporated into the design of the full-scale solution?
<--- Score

89. What improvements have been achieved?
<--- Score

90. When you map the key players in your own work and the types/domains of relationships with them, which relationships do you find easy and which challenging, and why?
<--- Score

91. How does the team improve its work?
<--- Score

92. Are the risks fully understood, reasonable and manageable?
<--- Score

93. Are events managed to resolution?
<--- Score

94. Who are the people involved in developing and implementing Improve Operation?
<--- Score

95. How do you link measurement and risk?
<--- Score

96. Do vendor agreements bring new compliance risk ?
<--- Score

97. How can the phases of Improve Operation development be identified?
<--- Score

98. Is Improve Operation documentation maintained?

<--- Score

99. Is supporting Improve Operation documentation required?
<--- Score

100. What are the implications of the one critical Improve Operation decision 10 minutes, 10 months, and 10 years from now?
<--- Score

101. How do you measure risk?
<--- Score

102. Who manages supplier risk management in your organization?
<--- Score

103. Is the Improve Operation solution sustainable?
<--- Score

104. How can you improve operational effectiveness and ROI?
<--- Score

105. What area needs the greatest improvement?
<--- Score

106. How do you improve operational efficiency?
<--- Score

107. To what extent does management recognize Improve Operation as a tool to increase the results?
<--- Score

108. What are the benefits of using OEE to improve

operational performance?
<--- Score

109. What is the team's contingency plan for potential problems occurring in implementation?
<--- Score

110. Are decisions made in a timely manner?
<--- Score

111. Do you cover the five essential competencies: Communication, Collaboration,Innovation, Adaptability, and Leadership that improve an organizations ability to leverage the new Improve Operation in a volatile global economy?
<--- Score

112. What is Improve Operation's impact on utilizing the best solution(s)?
<--- Score

113. Why improve in the first place?
<--- Score

114. Is the Improve Operation documentation thorough?
<--- Score

115. How will you measure the results?
<--- Score

116. Will the controls trigger any other risks?
<--- Score

117. What is the Improve Operation's sustainability risk?

<--- Score

118. What actually has to improve and by how much?
<--- Score

119. Explorations of the frontiers of Improve Operation will help you build influence, improve Improve Operation, optimize decision making, and sustain change, what is your approach?
<--- Score

120. What Improve Operation improvements can be made?
<--- Score

121. Have you identified breakpoints and/or risk tolerances that will trigger broad consideration of a potential need for intervention or modification of strategy?
<--- Score

122. How do you mitigate Improve Operation risk?
<--- Score

123. Do you combine technical expertise with business knowledge and Improve Operation Key topics include lifecycles, development approaches, requirements and how to make a business case?
<--- Score

124. Are you assessing Improve Operation and risk?
<--- Score

125. Which Improve Operation solution is appropriate?
<--- Score

126. How can skill-level changes improve Improve Operation?
<--- Score

127. How do you decide how much to remunerate an employee?
<--- Score

128. How can you better manage risk?
<--- Score

129. What is Improve Operation risk?
<--- Score

130. Risk events: what are the things that could go wrong?
<--- Score

131. How do you manage Improve Operation risk?
<--- Score

132. Have you achieved Improve Operation improvements?
<--- Score

133. How can you improve performance?
<--- Score

134. Do you need to do a usability evaluation?
<--- Score

Add up total points for this section:
_ _ _ _ _ = Total points for this section

Divided by: _ _ _ _ _ _ (number of

statements answered) = _____
Average score for this section

Transfer your score to the Improve
Operation Index at the beginning of the
Self-Assessment.

CRITERION #6: CONTROL:

INTENT: Implement the practical solution. Maintain the performance and correct possible complications.

In my belief, the answer to this question is clearly defined:

5 Strongly Agree

4 Agree

3 Neutral

2 Disagree

1 Strongly Disagree

1. Are the planned controls working?
<--- Score

2. How do you plan on providing proper recognition and disclosure of supporting companies?
<--- Score

3. What is your plan to assess your security risks?
<--- Score

4. Is there a control plan in place for sustaining improvements (short and long-term)?
<--- Score

5. What are the known security controls?
<--- Score

6. Does Improve Operation appropriately measure and monitor risk?
<--- Score

7. What is the best design framework for Improve Operation organization now that, in a post industrial-age if the top-down, command and control model is no longer relevant?
<--- Score

8. How do you plan for the cost of succession?
<--- Score

9. Has the Improve Operation value of standards been quantified?
<--- Score

10. Is there a standardized process?
<--- Score

11. How will the day-to-day responsibilities for monitoring and continual improvement be transferred from the improvement team to the process owner?
<--- Score

12. Have new or revised work instructions resulted?
<--- Score

13. How will report readings be checked to effectively monitor performance?
<--- Score

14. How can you best use all of your knowledge repositories to enhance learning and sharing?
<--- Score

15. Do the Improve Operation decisions you make today help people and the planet tomorrow?
<--- Score

16. What are your results for key measures or indicators of the accomplishment of your Improve Operation strategy and action plans, including building and strengthening core competencies?
<--- Score

17. Are suggested corrective/restorative actions indicated on the response plan for known causes to problems that might surface?
<--- Score

18. How do you select, collect, align, and integrate Improve Operation data and information for tracking daily operations and overall organizational performance, including progress relative to strategic objectives and action plans?
<--- Score

19. What quality tools were useful in the control phase?
<--- Score

20. Is there a Improve Operation Communication plan

covering who needs to get what information when?
<--- Score

21. How do senior leaders actions reflect a commitment to the organizations Improve Operation values?
<--- Score

22. Is there a transfer of ownership and knowledge to process owner and process team tasked with the responsibilities.
<--- Score

23. Who controls critical resources?
<--- Score

24. Is reporting being used or needed?
<--- Score

25. Are operating procedures consistent?
<--- Score

26. What other areas of the group might benefit from the Improve Operation team's improvements, knowledge, and learning?
<--- Score

27. What is the recommended frequency of auditing?
<--- Score

28. Is there documentation that will support the successful operation of the improvement?
<--- Score

29. What are the critical parameters to watch?
<--- Score

30. Does the response plan contain a definite closed loop continual improvement scheme (e.g., plan-do-check-act)?
<--- Score

31. Is the Improve Operation test/monitoring cost justified?
<--- Score

32. Who sets the Improve Operation standards?
<--- Score

33. Do you monitor the Improve Operation decisions made and fine tune them as they evolve?
<--- Score

34. Are new process steps, standards, and documentation ingrained into normal operations?
<--- Score

35. How is Improve Operation project cost planned, managed, monitored?
<--- Score

36. How widespread is its use?
<--- Score

37. What can you control?
<--- Score

38. What should you measure to verify efficiency gains?
<--- Score

39. How will you measure your QA plan's

effectiveness?
<--- Score

40. Will your goals reflect your program budget?
<--- Score

41. Are documented procedures clear and easy to follow for the operators?
<--- Score

42. Can support from partners be adjusted?
<--- Score

43. How might the group capture best practices and lessons learned so as to leverage improvements?
<--- Score

44. Are the planned controls in place?
<--- Score

45. How do you spread information?
<--- Score

46. Is a response plan in place for when the input, process, or output measures indicate an 'out-of-control' condition?
<--- Score

47. Is there an action plan in case of emergencies?
<--- Score

48. What do you measure to verify effectiveness gains?
<--- Score

49. Does the Improve Operation performance meet

the customer's requirements?
<--- Score

50. Is knowledge gained on process shared and institutionalized?
<--- Score

51. Are pertinent alerts monitored, analyzed and distributed to appropriate personnel?
<--- Score

52. What are you attempting to measure/monitor?
<--- Score

53. What do you stand for--and what are you against?
<--- Score

54. Do the viable solutions scale to future needs?
<--- Score

55. What is the standard for acceptable Improve Operation performance?
<--- Score

56. How is change control managed?
<--- Score

57. How will the process owner verify improvement in present and future sigma levels, process capabilities?
<--- Score

58. Is new knowledge gained imbedded in the response plan?
<--- Score

59. Is a response plan established and deployed?

<--- Score

60. How do you monitor usage and cost?
<--- Score

61. Will existing staff require re-training, for example, to learn new business processes?
<--- Score

62. What are customers monitoring?
<--- Score

63. How will Improve Operation decisions be made and monitored?
<--- Score

64. Where do ideas that reach policy makers and planners as proposals for Improve Operation strengthening and reform actually originate?
<--- Score

65. Will any special training be provided for results interpretation?
<--- Score

66. What should the next improvement project be that is related to Improve Operation?
<--- Score

67. Who is the Improve Operation process owner?
<--- Score

68. Does a troubleshooting guide exist or is it needed?
<--- Score

69. What other systems, operations, processes, and

infrastructures (hiring practices, staffing, training, incentives/rewards, metrics/dashboards/scorecards, etc.) need updates, additions, changes, or deletions in order to facilitate knowledge transfer and improvements?
<--- Score

70. Who has control over resources?
<--- Score

71. Are controls in place and consistently applied?
<--- Score

72. Can you adapt and adjust to changing Improve Operation situations?
<--- Score

73. Do you monitor the effectiveness of your Improve Operation activities?
<--- Score

74. Are there documented procedures?
<--- Score

75. What is the control/monitoring plan?
<--- Score

76. Does job training on the documented procedures need to be part of the process team's education and training?
<--- Score

77. What are the key elements of your Improve Operation performance improvement system, including your evaluation, organizational learning, and innovation processes?

<--- Score

78. How will the process owner and team be able to hold the gains?
<--- Score

79. Act/Adjust: What Do you Need to Do Differently?
<--- Score

80. What are the performance and scale of the Improve Operation tools?
<--- Score

81. Has the improved process and its steps been standardized?
<--- Score

82. How will input, process, and output variables be checked to detect for sub-optimal conditions?
<--- Score

83. Is there a recommended audit plan for routine surveillance inspections of Improve Operation's gains?
<--- Score

84. What key inputs and outputs are being measured on an ongoing basis?
<--- Score

85. What Improve Operation standards are applicable?
<--- Score

86. What adjustments to the strategies are needed?
<--- Score

87. How do controls support value?

<--- Score

88. How do your controls stack up?
<--- Score

89. Will the team be available to assist members in planning investigations?
<--- Score

90. Who will be in control?
<--- Score

91. How will new or emerging customer needs/ requirements be checked/communicated to orient the process toward meeting the new specifications and continually reducing variation?
<--- Score

92. What do your reports reflect?
<--- Score

93. Implementation Planning: is a pilot needed to test the changes before a full roll out occurs?
<--- Score

94. In the case of a Improve Operation project, the criteria for the audit derive from implementation objectives, an audit of a Improve Operation project involves assessing whether the recommendations outlined for implementation have been met, can you track that any Improve Operation project is implemented as planned, and is it working?
<--- Score

95. Are you measuring, monitoring and predicting Improve Operation activities to optimize operations

and profitability, and enhancing outcomes?
<--- Score

96. How do you establish and deploy modified action plans if circumstances require a shift in plans and rapid execution of new plans?
<--- Score

97. Who is going to spread your message?
<--- Score

98. Is there a documented and implemented monitoring plan?
<--- Score

99. Are the Improve Operation standards challenging?
<--- Score

Add up total points for this section:
_ _ _ _ _ = Total points for this section

Divided by: _ _ _ _ _ _ (number of statements answered) = _ _ _ _ _ _
Average score for this section

Transfer your score to the Improve Operation Index at the beginning of the Self-Assessment.

CRITERION #7: SUSTAIN:

INTENT: Retain the benefits.

In my belief, the answer to this question is clearly defined:

5 Strongly Agree

4 Agree

3 Neutral

2 Disagree

1 Strongly Disagree

1. Who is on the team?
<--- Score

2. In retrospect, of the projects that you pulled the plug on, what percent do you wish had been allowed to keep going, and what percent do you wish had ended earlier?
<--- Score

3. How do you create buy-in?
<--- Score

4. If your customer were your grandmother, would you tell her to buy what you're selling?
<--- Score

5. What must you excel at?
<--- Score

6. How do you deal with Improve Operation changes?
<--- Score

7. What relationships among Improve Operation trends do you perceive?
<--- Score

8. When information truly is ubiquitous, when reach and connectivity are completely global, when computing resources are infinite, and when a whole new set of impossibilities are not only possible, but happening, what will that do to your business?
<--- Score

9. What Improve Operation skills are most important?
<--- Score

10. How do you proactively clarify deliverables and Improve Operation quality expectations?
<--- Score

11. In the past year, what have you done (or could you have done) to increase the accurate perception of your company/brand as ethical and honest?
<--- Score

12. Why not do Improve Operation?
<--- Score

13. Did your employees make progress today?
<--- Score

14. What are the potential basics of Improve Operation fraud?
<--- Score

15. Which models, tools and techniques are necessary?
<--- Score

16. Do you have the right capabilities and capacities?
<--- Score

17. Are you changing as fast as the world around you?
<--- Score

18. Marketing budgets are tighter, consumers are more skeptical, and social media has changed forever the way we talk about Improve Operation, how do you gain traction?
<--- Score

19. Is your basic point _____ or _____?
<--- Score

20. How do you stay inspired?
<--- Score

21. How long will it take to change?
<--- Score

22. Who is the main stakeholder, with ultimate responsibility for driving Improve Operation forward?
<--- Score

23. Think of your Improve Operation project, what are the main functions?
<--- Score

24. Are the criteria for selecting recommendations stated?
<--- Score

25. How do you assess the Improve Operation pitfalls that are inherent in implementing it?
<--- Score

26. Can you maintain your growth without detracting from the factors that have contributed to your success?
<--- Score

27. What are the challenges?
<--- Score

28. What are the long-term Improve Operation goals?
<--- Score

29. Political -is anyone trying to undermine this project?
<--- Score

30. What trouble can you get into?
<--- Score

31. How much contingency will be available in the budget?
<--- Score

32. Is there any reason to believe the opposite of my

current belief?
<--- Score

33. What is the estimated value of the project?
<--- Score

34. If you weren't already in this business, would you enter it today? And if not, what are you going to do about it?
<--- Score

35. Who is responsible for Improve Operation?
<--- Score

36. What is the recommended frequency of auditing?
<--- Score

37. Are you using a design thinking approach and integrating Innovation, Improve Operation Experience, and Brand Value?
<--- Score

38. How is implementation research currently incorporated into each of your goals?
<--- Score

39. What are you challenging?
<--- Score

40. What you are going to do to affect the numbers?
<--- Score

41. What is your formula for success in Improve Operation ?
<--- Score

42. If there were zero limitations, what would you do differently?
<--- Score

43. Who will determine interim and final deadlines?
<--- Score

44. What is the purpose of Improve Operation in relation to the mission?
<--- Score

45. What are you trying to prove to yourself, and how might it be hijacking your life and business success?
<--- Score

46. How do senior leaders deploy your organizations vision and values through your leadership system, to the workforce, to key suppliers and partners, and to customers and other stakeholders, as appropriate?
<--- Score

47. Who will be responsible for deciding whether Improve Operation goes ahead or not after the initial investigations?
<--- Score

48. Who do we want your customers to become?
<--- Score

49. Why is it important to have senior management support for a Improve Operation project?
<--- Score

50. What happens if you do not have enough funding?
<--- Score

51. Is your strategy driving your strategy? Or is the way in which you allocate resources driving your strategy?
<--- Score

52. Who are your customers?
<--- Score

53. How do you make it meaningful in connecting Improve Operation with what users do day-to-day?
<--- Score

54. What are the essentials of internal Improve Operation management?
<--- Score

55. How do you provide a safe environment -physically and emotionally?
<--- Score

56. What is the overall business strategy?
<--- Score

57. Instead of going to current contacts for new ideas, what if you reconnected with dormant contacts-- the people you used to know? If you were going reactivate a dormant tie, who would it be?
<--- Score

58. How do you keep the momentum going?
<--- Score

59. What is the source of the strategies for Improve Operation strengthening and reform?
<--- Score

60. What are specific Improve Operation rules to follow?
<--- Score

61. What goals did you miss?
<--- Score

62. How will you know that the Improve Operation project has been successful?
<--- Score

63. Which individuals, teams or departments will be involved in Improve Operation?
<--- Score

64. What is your competitive advantage?
<--- Score

65. If you were responsible for initiating and implementing major changes in your organization, what steps might you take to ensure acceptance of those changes?
<--- Score

66. How do you determine the key elements that affect Improve Operation workforce satisfaction, how are these elements determined for different workforce groups and segments?
<--- Score

67. What is the kind of project structure that would be appropriate for your Improve Operation project, should it be formal and complex, or can it be less formal and relatively simple?
<--- Score

68. Why should people listen to you?
<--- Score

69. Who uses your product in ways you never expected?
<--- Score

70. What business benefits will Improve Operation goals deliver if achieved?
<--- Score

71. Operational - will it work?
<--- Score

72. Is there a work around that you can use?
<--- Score

73. What happens at your organization when people fail?
<--- Score

74. What are the rules and assumptions your industry operates under? What if the opposite were true?
<--- Score

75. If you had to rebuild your organization without any traditional competitive advantages (i.e., no killer technology, promising research, innovative product/ service delivery model, etcetera), how would your people have to approach their work and collaborate together in order to create the necessary conditions for success?
<--- Score

76. What are the barriers to increased Improve

Operation production?
<--- Score

77. What is the overall talent health of your organization as a whole at senior levels, and for each organization reporting to a member of the Senior Leadership Team?
<--- Score

78. Is maximizing Improve Operation protection the same as minimizing Improve Operation loss?
<--- Score

79. What would you recommend your friend do if he/she were facing this dilemma?
<--- Score

80. What was the last experiment you ran?
<--- Score

81. Is it economical; do you have the time and money?
<--- Score

82. Where can you break convention?
<--- Score

83. What is the funding source for this project?
<--- Score

84. How do you go about securing Improve Operation?
<--- Score

85. Who are four people whose careers you have enhanced?
<--- Score

86. What potential megatrends could make your business model obsolete?
<--- Score

87. How can you incorporate support to ensure safe and effective use of Improve Operation into the services that you provide?
<--- Score

88. If you got fired and a new hire took your place, what would she do different?
<--- Score

89. What are your personal philosophies regarding Improve Operation and how do they influence your work?
<--- Score

90. Do you know what you are doing? And who do you call if you don't?
<--- Score

91. What are internal and external Improve Operation relations?
<--- Score

92. How will you insure seamless interoperability of Improve Operation moving forward?
<--- Score

93. How important is Improve Operation to the user organizations mission?
<--- Score

94. How do you maintain Improve Operation's

Integrity?

<--- Score

95. Which functions and people interact with the supplier and or customer?

<--- Score

96. Is Improve Operation realistic, or are you setting yourself up for failure?

<--- Score

97. Who have you, as a company, historically been when you've been at your best?

<--- Score

98. Are you satisfied with your current role? If not, what is missing from it?

<--- Score

99. Do you have the right people on the bus?

<--- Score

100. How do you transition from the baseline to the target?

<--- Score

101. Do you have an implicit bias for capital investments over people investments?

<--- Score

102. What new services of functionality will be implemented next with Improve Operation ?

<--- Score

103. Can you do all this work?

<--- Score

104. Do you feel that more should be done in the Improve Operation area?
<--- Score

105. What is something you believe that nearly no one agrees with you on?
<--- Score

106. What management system can you use to leverage the Improve Operation experience, ideas, and concerns of the people closest to the work to be done?
<--- Score

107. If you had to leave your organization for a year and the only communication you could have with employees/colleagues was a single paragraph, what would you write?
<--- Score

108. What is an unauthorized commitment?
<--- Score

109. How will you motivate the stakeholders with the least vested interest?
<--- Score

110. How will you ensure you get what you expected?
<--- Score

111. Is Improve Operation dependent on the successful delivery of a current project?
<--- Score

112. What information is critical to your organization

that your executives are ignoring?
<--- Score

113. Are you relevant? Will you be relevant five years from now? Ten?
<--- Score

114. Do you have past Improve Operation successes?
<--- Score

115. What should you stop doing?
<--- Score

116. To whom do you add value?
<--- Score

117. What did you miss in the interview for the worst hire you ever made?
<--- Score

118. Which Improve Operation goals are the most important?
<--- Score

119. What are the key enablers to make this Improve Operation move?
<--- Score

120. What happens when a new employee joins the organization?
<--- Score

121. What are strategies for increasing support and reducing opposition?
<--- Score

122. How do you accomplish your long range Improve Operation goals?
<--- Score

123. What counts that you are not counting?
<--- Score

124. In a project to restructure Improve Operation outcomes, which stakeholders would you involve?
<--- Score

125. Do you see more potential in people than they do in themselves?
<--- Score

126. How can you become more high-tech but still be high touch?
<--- Score

127. What could happen if you do not do it?
<--- Score

128. What is the craziest thing you can do?
<--- Score

129. Can the schedule be done in the given time?
<--- Score

130. Whom among your colleagues do you trust, and for what?
<--- Score

131. What is your question? Why?
<--- Score

132. Who, on the executive team or the board, has

spoken to a customer recently?
<--- Score

133. What does your signature ensure?
<--- Score

134. Is a Improve Operation team work effort in place?
<--- Score

135. If you find that you havent accomplished one of the goals for one of the steps of the Improve Operation strategy, what will you do to fix it?
<--- Score

136. What one word do you want to own in the minds of your customers, employees, and partners?
<--- Score

137. Who are the key stakeholders?
<--- Score

138. How do you cross-sell and up-sell your Improve Operation success?
<--- Score

139. Why will customers want to buy your organizations products/services?
<--- Score

140. What is it like to work for you?
<--- Score

141. Are all key stakeholders present at all Structured Walkthroughs?
<--- Score

142. At what moment would you think; Will I get fired?
<--- Score

143. How do you keep records, of what?
<--- Score

144. If your company went out of business tomorrow, would anyone who doesn't get a paycheck here care?
<--- Score

145. What Improve Operation modifications can you make work for you?
<--- Score

146. What knowledge, skills and characteristics mark a good Improve Operation project manager?
<--- Score

147. How do you lead with Improve Operation in mind?
<--- Score

148. How do you foster innovation?
<--- Score

149. What will be the consequences to the stakeholder (financial, reputation etc) if Improve Operation does not go ahead or fails to deliver the objectives?
<--- Score

150. Do you say no to customers for no reason?
<--- Score

151. How do you foster the skills, knowledge, talents, attributes, and characteristics you want to have?

<--- Score

152. What is the range of capabilities?
<--- Score

153. What are the gaps in your knowledge and experience?
<--- Score

154. What may be the consequences for the performance of an organization if all stakeholders are not consulted regarding Improve Operation?
<--- Score

155. Do you have enough freaky customers in your portfolio pushing you to the limit day in and day out?
<--- Score

156. How can you negotiate Improve Operation successfully with a stubborn boss, an irate client, or a deceitful coworker?
<--- Score

157. What trophy do you want on your mantle?
<--- Score

158. What role does communication play in the success or failure of a Improve Operation project?
<--- Score

159. What are the short and long-term Improve Operation goals?
<--- Score

160. Why do and why don't your customers like your organization?

<--- Score

161. How do you ensure that implementations of Improve Operation products are done in a way that ensures safety?
<--- Score

162. How do you set Improve Operation stretch targets and how do you get people to not only participate in setting these stretch targets but also that they strive to achieve these?
<--- Score

163. Are you / should you be revolutionary or evolutionary?
<--- Score

164. Who is responsible for ensuring appropriate resources (time, people and money) are allocated to Improve Operation?
<--- Score

165. What is your BATNA (best alternative to a negotiated agreement)?
<--- Score

166. What unique value proposition (UVP) do you offer?
<--- Score

167. How are you doing compared to your industry?
<--- Score

168. How do you govern and fulfill your societal responsibilities?
<--- Score

169. What is a feasible sequencing of reform initiatives over time?
<--- Score

170. What are the top 3 things at the forefront of your Improve Operation agendas for the next 3 years?
<--- Score

171. Are you paying enough attention to the partners your company depends on to succeed?
<--- Score

172. What is effective Improve Operation?
<--- Score

173. What is your Improve Operation strategy?
<--- Score

174. Do you think you know, or do you know you know ?
<--- Score

175. What are your most important goals for the strategic Improve Operation objectives?
<--- Score

176. Do you think Improve Operation accomplishes the goals you expect it to accomplish?
<--- Score

177. Has implementation been effective in reaching specified objectives so far?
<--- Score

178. Who will provide the final approval of Improve

Operation deliverables?
<--- Score

179. Are you maintaining a past–present–future perspective throughout the Improve Operation discussion?
<--- Score

180. Is the Improve Operation organization completing tasks effectively and efficiently?
<--- Score

181. How can you become the company that would put you out of business?
<--- Score

182. Is there any existing Improve Operation governance structure?
<--- Score

183. How do customers see your organization?
<--- Score

184. Why is Improve Operation important for you now?
<--- Score

185. Are assumptions made in Improve Operation stated explicitly?
<--- Score

186. What have you done to protect your business from competitive encroachment?
<--- Score

187. Would you rather sell to knowledgeable and

informed customers or to uninformed customers?
<--- Score

188. How do you listen to customers to obtain actionable information?
<--- Score

189. Will it be accepted by users?
<--- Score

Add up total points for this section:
_ _ _ _ _ = Total points for this section

Divided by: _ _ _ _ _ _ (number of statements answered) = _ _ _ _ _ _
Average score for this section

Transfer your score to the Improve Operation Index at the beginning of the Self-Assessment.

Improve Operation and Managing Projects, Criteria for Project Managers:

1.0 Initiating Process Group: Improve Operation

1. How to control and approve each phase?

2. What will be the pressing issues of tomorrow?

3. What do they need to know about the Improve Operation project?

4. When will the Improve Operation project be done?

5. How do you help others satisfy needs?

6. During which stage of Risk planning are modeling techniques used to determine overall effects of risks on Improve Operation project objectives for high probability, high impact risks?

7. Were resources available as planned?

8. Professionals want to know what is expected from them what are the deliverables?

9. Are you just doing busywork to pass the time?

10. What is the stake of others in your Improve Operation project?

11. Will the Improve Operation project meet the client requirements, and will it achieve the business success criteria that justified doing the Improve Operation project in the first place?

12. Do you understand all business (operational),

technical, resource and vendor risks associated with the Improve Operation project?

13. First of all, should any action be taken?

14. Do you know the Improve Operation projects goal, purpose and objectives?

15. How well did you do?

16. Although the Improve Operation project manager does not directly manage procurement and contracting activities, who does manage procurement and contracting activities in your organization then if not the PM?

17. What are the overarching issues of your organization?

18. Have the stakeholders identified all individual requirements pertaining to business process?

19. What technical work to do in each phase?

20. Have you evaluated the teams performance and asked for feedback?

1.1 Project Charter: Improve Operation

21. Pop quiz – which are the same inputs as in the Improve Operation project charter?

22. What date will the task finish?

23. Who is the Improve Operation project Manager?

24. Why use a Improve Operation project charter?

25. Avoid costs, improve service, and/ or comply with a mandate?

26. Where does all this information come from?

27. Who will take notes, document decisions?

28. Are there special technology requirements?

29. What is the most common tool for helping define the detail?

30. What is the purpose of the Improve Operation project?

31. What are the known stakeholder requirements?

32. Assumptions: what factors, for planning purposes, are you considering to be true?

33. What are you trying to accomplish?

34. Review the general mission What system will be affected by the improvement efforts?

35. How much?

36. Will this replace an existing product?

37. For whom?

38. Does the Improve Operation project need to consider any special capacity or capability issues?

39. If finished, on what date did it finish?

40. Fit with other Products Compliments – Cannibalizes?

1.2 Stakeholder Register: Improve Operation

41. What opportunities exist to provide communications?

42. What is the power of the stakeholder?

43. Is your organization ready for change?

44. How big is the gap?

45. How should employers make voices heard?

46. Who is managing stakeholder engagement?

47. How will reports be created?

48. Who are the stakeholders?

49. What & Why?

50. Who wants to talk about Security?

51. What are the major Improve Operation project milestones requiring communications or providing communications opportunities?

52. How much influence do they have on the Improve Operation project?

1.3 Stakeholder Analysis Matrix: Improve Operation

53. Which conditions out of the control of the management are crucial for the sustainability of its effects?

54. Geographical, export, import?

55. What do you Evaluate?

56. Market demand?

57. How do you manage Improve Operation project Risk?

58. How do customers express needs?

59. Disadvantages of proposition?

60. Economy - home, abroad?

61. How can you fill the need to show progress?

62. How are the threatened Improve Operation project targets being used?

63. Sustaining internal capabilities?

64. Beneficiaries; who are the potential beneficiaries?

65. How can you counter negative efforts?

66. Niche target markets?

67. Is changing technology threatening your organizations position?

68. What is the stakeholders power and status in relation to the Improve Operation project?

69. How to involve media?

70. New technologies, services, ideas?

71. Which resources are required?

72. Benefit to whom?

2.0 Planning Process Group: Improve Operation

73. How well do the team follow the chosen processes?

74. What do you need to do?

75. Did you read it correctly?

76. Is the duration of the program sufficient to ensure a cycle that will Improve Operation project the sustainability of the interventions?

77. What is the critical path for this Improve Operation project, and what is the duration of the critical path?

78. What is involved in Improve Operation project scope management, and why is good Improve Operation project scope management so important on information technology Improve Operation projects?

79. To what extent is the program helping to influence your organizations policy framework?

80. What type of estimation method are you using?

81. Is the Improve Operation project supported by national and/or local organizations?

82. In what way has the Improve Operation project come up with innovative measures for problem-

solving?

83. What makes your Improve Operation project successful?

84. How well defined and documented are the Improve Operation project management processes you chose to use?

85. Is the pace of implementing the products of the program ensuring the completeness of the results of the Improve Operation project?

86. Did the program design/ implementation strategy adequately address the planning stage necessary to set up structures, hire staff etc.?

87. Will the products created live up to the necessary quality?

88. To what extent has a PMO contributed to raising the quality of the design of the Improve Operation project?

89. What are the different approaches to building the WBS?

90. Is the identification of the problems, inequalities and gaps, with respective causes, clear in the Improve Operation project?

91. Is your organization showing technical capacity and leadership commitment to keep working with the Improve Operation project and to repeat it?

92. To what extent have public/private national

resources and/or counterparts been mobilized to contribute to the programs objective and produce results and impacts?

2.1 Project Management Plan: Improve Operation

93. What are the assigned resources?

94. Are there any scope changes proposed for a previously authorized Improve Operation project?

95. Has the selected plan been formulated using cost effectiveness and incremental analysis techniques?

96. What would you do differently?

97. What are the constraints?

98. Is mitigation authorized or recommended?

99. How well are you able to manage your risk?

100. Are there any windfall benefits that would accrue to the Improve Operation project sponsor or other parties?

101. What are the deliverables?

102. How do you organize the costs in the Improve Operation project management plan?

103. What are the training needs?

104. If the Improve Operation project is complex or scope is specialized, do you have appropriate and/or qualified staff available to perform the tasks?

105. What data/reports/tools/etc. do program managers need?

106. Is there an incremental analysis/cost effectiveness analysis of proposed mitigation features based on an approved method and using an accepted model?

107. What went right?

108. Is there anything you would now do differently on your Improve Operation project based on past experience?

109. What did not work so well?

110. Who manages integration?

2.2 Scope Management Plan: Improve Operation

111. Is quality monitored from the perspective of the customers needs and expectations?

112. Will your organizations estimating methodology be used and followed?

113. Cost / benefit analysis?

114. Is there a formal process for updating the Improve Operation project baseline?

115. Is there a Steering Committee in place?

116. Are staff skills known and available for each task?

117. Are vendor contract reports, reviews and visits conducted periodically?

118. Have Improve Operation project success criteria been defined?

119. Sensitivity analysis?

120. Assess the expected stability of the scope of this Improve Operation project how likely is it to change, how frequently, and by how much?

121. Is there a formal set of procedures supporting Issues Management?

122. What are the risks that could significantly affect the resources needed for the Improve Operation project?

123. Does the detailed work plan match the complexity of tasks with the capabilities of personnel?

124. What are the acceptance criteria (process and criteria to be met for key stakeholder acceptance) and who is authorized to sign off?

125. Are there any scope changes proposed for the previously authorized Improve Operation project?

126. Has the Improve Operation project scope been baselined?

127. Are funding resource estimates sufficiently detailed and documented for use in planning and tracking the Improve Operation project?

128. Describe the process for rejecting the Improve Operation project deliverables. What happens to rejected deliverables?

129. Time estimation – how much time will be needed?

130. Personnel with expertise?

2.3 Requirements Management Plan: Improve Operation

131. Will the Improve Operation project requirements become approved in writing?

132. Do you have price sheets and a methodology for determining the total proposal cost?

133. Is the system software (non-operating system) new to the IT Improve Operation project team?

134. Did you avoid subjective, flowery or non-specific statements?

135. Who will approve the requirements (and if multiple approvers, in what order)?

136. How do you know that you have done this right?

137. Is any organizational data being used or stored?

138. Do you know which stakeholders will participate in the requirements effort?

139. Is it new or replacing an existing business system or process?

140. Will the contractors involved take full responsibility?

141. Is there formal agreement on who has authority to approve a change in requirements?

142. Who is responsible for quantifying the Improve Operation project requirements?

143. Should you include sub-activities?

144. Who will perform the analysis?

145. How will you develop the schedule of requirements activities?

146. How detailed should the Improve Operation project get?

147. Has the requirements team been instructed in the Change Control process?

148. Will you use tracing to help understand the impact of a change in requirements?

149. If it exists, where is it housed?

150. Have stakeholders been instructed in the Change Control process?

2.4 Requirements Documentation: Improve Operation

151. What images does it conjure?

152. What are the attributes of a customer?

153. What can tools do for us?

154. Are there legal issues?

155. Are all functions required by the customer included?

156. If applicable; are there issues linked with the fact that this is an offshore Improve Operation project?

157. Who is interacting with the system?

158. Does the system provide the functions which best support the customers needs?

159. How will the proposed Improve Operation project help?

160. What marketing channels do you want to use: e-mail, letter or sms?

161. How linear / iterative is your Requirements Gathering process (or will it be)?

162. What is the risk associated with cost and schedule?

163. Do your constraints stand?

164. Can you check system requirements?

165. Is your business case still valid?

166. How will they be documented / shared?

167. Who provides requirements?

168. What facilities must be supported by the system?

169. Where do you define what is a customer, what are the attributes of customer?

170. Basic work/business process; high-level, what is being touched?

2.5 Requirements Traceability Matrix: Improve Operation

171. Is there a requirements traceability process in place?

172. Why do you manage scope?

173. What is the WBS?

174. Describe the process for approving requirements so they can be added to the traceability matrix and Improve Operation project work can be performed. Will the Improve Operation project requirements become approved in writing?

175. Why use a WBS?

176. What are the chronologies, contingencies, consequences, criteria?

177. Will you use a Requirements Traceability Matrix?

178. How small is small enough?

179. Do you have a clear understanding of all subcontracts in place?

180. What percentage of Improve Operation projects are producing traceability matrices between requirements and other work products?

181. How will it affect the stakeholders personally in

career?

182. How do you manage scope?

2.6 Project Scope Statement: Improve Operation

183. Elements of scope management that deal with concept development ?

184. Will all Improve Operation project issues be unconditionally tracked through the issue resolution process?

185. Are there adequate Improve Operation project control systems?

186. If there are vendors, have they signed off on the Improve Operation project Plan?

187. What is the product of this Improve Operation project?

188. What is a process you might recommend to verify the accuracy of the research deliverable?

189. Why do you need to manage scope?

190. Have you been able to easily identify success criteria and create objective measurements for each of the Improve Operation project scopes goal statements?

191. How often will scope changes be reviewed?

192. Have you been able to thoroughly document the Improve Operation projects assumptions and

constraints?

193. Are the input requirements from the team members clearly documented and communicated?

194. Will tasks be marked complete only after QA has been successfully completed?

195. Will the risk documents be filed?

196. Once its defined, what is the stability of the Improve Operation project scope?

197. Is the Improve Operation project manager qualified and experienced in Improve Operation project management?

198. Relevant - ask yourself can you get there; why are you doing this Improve Operation project?

199. Will you need a statement of work?

200. Were potential customers involved early in the planning process?

2.7 Assumption and Constraint Log: Improve Operation

201. Have the scope, objectives, costs, benefits and impacts been communicated to all involved and/or impacted stakeholders and work groups?

202. No superfluous information or marketing narrative?

203. Has the approach and development strategy of the Improve Operation project been defined, documented and accepted by the appropriate stakeholders?

204. What is positive about the current process?

205. Does the document/deliverable meet all requirements (for example, statement of work) specific to this deliverable?

206. Would known impacts serve as impediments?

207. What do you log?

208. Do documented requirements exist for all critical components and areas, including technical, business, interfaces, performance, security and conversion requirements?

209. Have all stakeholders been identified?

210. Are there standards for code development?

211. How can constraints be violated?

212. When can log be discarded?

213. Does the plan conform to standards?

214. Is the process working, and people are not executing in compliance of the process?

215. Model-building: what data-analytic strategies are useful when building proportional-hazards models?

216. Does the traceability documentation describe the tool and/or mechanism to be used to capture traceability throughout the life cycle?

217. How are new requirements or changes to requirements identified?

218. How relevant is this attribute to this Improve Operation project or audit?

219. Were the system requirements formally reviewed prior to initiating the design phase?

2.8 Work Breakdown Structure: Improve Operation

220. Where does it take place?

221. What is the probability that the Improve Operation project duration will exceed xx weeks?

222. Is the work breakdown structure (wbs) defined and is the scope of the Improve Operation project clear with assigned deliverable owners?

223. Who has to do it?

224. How big is a work-package?

225. What is the probability of completing the Improve Operation project in less that xx days?

226. How far down?

227. What has to be done?

228. Is it still viable?

229. When does it have to be done?

230. How will you and your Improve Operation project team define the Improve Operation projects scope and work breakdown structure?

231. Why would you develop a Work Breakdown Structure?

232. Do you need another level?

233. Is it a change in scope?

234. How much detail?

235. Can you make it?

236. When do you stop?

2.9 WBS Dictionary: Improve Operation

237. The already stated responsible for overhead performance control of related costs?

238. Are the bases and rates for allocating costs from each indirect pool consistently applied?

239. Is work progressively subdivided into detailed work packages as requirements are defined?

240. Is budgeted cost for work performed calculated in a manner consistent with the way work is planned?

241. Do the lines of authority for incurring indirect costs correspond to the lines of responsibility for management control of the same components of costs?

242. Software specification, development, integration, and testing, licenses ?

243. Time-phased control account budgets?

244. Are the procedures for identifying indirect costs to incurring organizations, indirect cost pools, and allocating the costs from the pools to the contracts formally documented?

245. Are internal budgets for authorized, and not priced changes based on the contractors resource plan for accomplishing the work?

246. Does the contractors system include procedures for measuring performance of the lowest level organization responsible for the control account?

247. Are management actions taken to reduce indirect costs when there are significant adverse variances?

248. Identify potential or actual overruns and underruns?

249. What should you drop in order to add something new?

250. Where learning is used in developing underlying budgets is there a direct relationship between anticipated learning and time phased budgets?

251. Do work packages reflect the actual way in which the work will be done and are they meaningful products or management-oriented subdivisions of a higher level element of work?

252. How detailed should a Improve Operation project get?

253. Actual cost of work performed?

254. Intermediate schedules, as required, which provide a logical sequence from the master schedule to the control account level?

255. Are the bases and rates for allocating costs from each indirect pool to commercial work consistent with the already stated used to allocate corresponding

costs to Government contracts?

2.10 Schedule Management Plan: Improve Operation

256. Are Improve Operation project leaders committed to this Improve Operation project full time?

257. Will the tools selected accomplish the scheduling needs?

258. Are the constraints or deadlines associated with the task accurate?

259. Are issues raised, assessed, actioned, and resolved in a timely and efficient manner?

260. Is a pmo (Improve Operation project management office) in place and provide oversight to the Improve Operation project?

261. Are action items captured and managed?

262. Has a Improve Operation project Communications Plan been developed?

263. Is there a formal process for updating the Improve Operation project baseline?

264. Have all involved Improve Operation project stakeholders and work groups committed to the Improve Operation project?

265. What weaknesses do you have?

266. Have activity relationships and interdependencies within tasks been adequately identified?

267. Are changes in deliverable commitments agreed to by all affected groups & individuals?

268. Is the plan consistent with industry best practices?

269. Have the key functions and capabilities been defined and assigned to each release or iteration?

270. Has a resource management plan been created?

271. Timeline and milestones?

272. Is there an issues management plan in place?

273. Was your organizations estimating methodology being used and followed?

274. Are trade-offs between accepting the risk and mitigating the risk identified?

2.11 Activity List: Improve Operation

275. How difficult will it be to do specific activities on this Improve Operation project?

276. How much slack is available in the Improve Operation project?

277. Where will it be performed?

278. Who will perform the work?

279. How will it be performed?

280. What are the critical bottleneck activities?

281. How should ongoing costs be monitored to try to keep the Improve Operation project within budget?

282. What went well?

283. What is the LF and LS for each activity?

284. What will be performed?

285. When do the individual activities need to start and finish?

286. Is there anything planned that does not need to be here?

287. Is infrastructure setup part of your Improve Operation project?

288. What is the total time required to complete the Improve Operation project if no delays occur?

289. For other activities, how much delay can be tolerated?

290. Can you determine the activity that must finish, before this activity can start?

291. Are the required resources available or need to be acquired?

292. What went wrong?

293. What did not go as well?

2.12 Activity Attributes: Improve Operation

294. Has management defined a definite timeframe for the turnaround or Improve Operation project window?

295. How much activity detail is required?

296. Have you identified the Activity Leveling Priority code value on each activity?

297. Time for overtime?

298. What is missing?

299. What is your organizations history in doing similar activities?

300. Have constraints been applied to the start and finish milestones for the phases?

301. How else could the items be grouped?

302. What activity do you think you should spend the most time on?

303. What conclusions/generalizations can you draw from this?

304. How difficult will it be to complete specific activities on this Improve Operation project?

305. How many resources do you need to complete the work scope within a limit of X number of days?

306. Activity: what is In the Bag?

307. Can you re-assign any activities to another resource to resolve an over-allocation?

308. Where else does it apply?

309. Is there a trend during the year?

310. Which method produces the more accurate cost assignment?

311. Activity: fair or not fair?

2.13 Milestone List: Improve Operation

312. What has been done so far?

313. Level of the Innovation?

314. Global influences?

315. Effects on core activities, distraction?

316. How will the milestone be verified?

317. Legislative effects?

318. What would happen if a delivery of material was one week late?

319. It is to be a narrative text providing the crucial aspects of your Improve Operation project proposal answering what, who, how, when and where?

320. Can you derive how soon can the whole Improve Operation project finish?

321. How late can each activity be finished and started?

322. Which path is the critical path?

323. How will you get the word out to customers?

324. Own known vulnerabilities?

325. Identify critical paths (one or more) and which activities are on the critical path?

326. Vital contracts and partners?

327. Describe the industry you are in and the market growth opportunities. What is the market for your technology, product or service?

328. Do you foresee any technical risks or developmental challenges?

329. Describe the concept of the technology, product or service that will be or has been developed. How will it be used?

2.14 Network Diagram: Improve Operation

330. What job or jobs follow it?

331. What is the lowest cost to complete this Improve Operation project in xx weeks?

332. Are the required resources available?

333. Can you calculate the confidence level?

334. Where do schedules come from?

335. How confident can you be in your milestone dates and the delivery date?

336. What activities must occur simultaneously with this activity?

337. How difficult will it be to do specific activities on this Improve Operation project?

338. Will crashing x weeks return more in benefits than it costs?

339. Why must you schedule milestones, such as reviews, throughout the Improve Operation project?

340. Are you on time?

341. What controls the start and finish of a job?

342. What is the completion time?

343. Where do you schedule uncertainty time?

344. Review the logical flow of the network diagram. Take a look at which activities you have first and then sequence the activities. Do they make sense?

345. What is the probability of completing the Improve Operation project in less that xx days?

346. Exercise: what is the probability that the Improve Operation project duration will exceed xx weeks?

347. What job or jobs could run concurrently?

348. What are the tools?

2.15 Activity Resource Requirements: Improve Operation

349. Organizational Applicability?

350. Anything else?

351. What is the Work Plan Standard?

352. Why do you do that?

353. How do you manage time?

354. Other support in specific areas?

355. How do you handle petty cash?

356. Are there unresolved issues that need to be addressed?

357. Do you use tools like decomposition and rolling-wave planning to produce the activity list and other outputs?

358. How many signatures do you require on a check and does this match what is in your policy and procedures?

359. When does monitoring begin?

360. What are constraints that you might find during the Human Resource Planning process?

361. Which logical relationship does the PDM use most often?

2.16 Resource Breakdown Structure: Improve Operation

362. The list could probably go on, but, the thing that you would most like to know is, How long & How much?

363. Why do you do it?

364. What can you do to improve productivity?

365. Goals for the Improve Operation project. What is each stakeholders desired outcome for the Improve Operation project?

366. Who will use the system?

367. Who needs what information?

368. Why is this important?

369. What defines a successful Improve Operation project?

370. Why time management?

371. What is the difference between % Complete and % work?

372. What defines a successful Improve Operation project?

373. When do they need the information?

374. Any changes from stakeholders?

375. How can this help you with team building?

376. Which resource planning tool provides information on resource responsibility and accountability?

377. What is each stakeholders desired outcome for the Improve Operation project?

378. Changes based on input from stakeholders?

2.17 Activity Duration Estimates: Improve Operation

379. Are actual Improve Operation project results compared with planned or expected results to determine the variance?

380. Find an example of a contract for information technology services. Analyze the key features of the contract. What type of contract was used and why?

381. Will it help promote wellness at your organization and reduce insurance costs?

382. Which frame seemed to be the most important and why?

383. How could you use each technique in your organization?

384. Which tips for taking the PMP exam do you think would be most helpful for you?

385. Is training acquired to enhance the skills, knowledge and capabilities of the Improve Operation project team?

386. Are changes to the scope managed according to defined procedures?

387. Do procedures exist describing how the Improve Operation project scope will be managed?

388. Why do you think schedule issues often cause the most conflicts on Improve Operation projects?

389. How do functionality, system outputs, performance, reliability, and maintainability requirements affect quality planning?

390. Is action taken to increase the effectiveness and efficiency of Improve Operation projects?

391. How do theories relate to Improve Operation project management?

392. Consider the examples of poor quality in information technology Improve Operation projects presented in the What Went Wrong?

393. What are the nine areas of expertise?

394. Is a standard form used to obtain bids and proposals from prospective sellers?

395. Are procedures defined for calculating cost estimates?

396. What type of information goes in a quality assurance plan?

397. How does the job market and current state of the economy affect human resource management?

398. Is earned value analysis completed to assess Improve Operation project performance?

2.18 Duration Estimating Worksheet: Improve Operation

399. What questions do you have?

400. What is an Average Improve Operation project?

401. Is the Improve Operation project responsive to community need?

402. Small or large Improve Operation project?

403. How should ongoing costs be monitored to try to keep the Improve Operation project within budget?

404. What info is needed?

405. Does the Improve Operation project provide innovative ways for stakeholders to overcome obstacles or deliver better outcomes?

406. Done before proceeding with this activity or what can be done concurrently?

407. Can the Improve Operation project be constructed as planned?

408. Will the Improve Operation project collaborate with the local community and leverage resources?

409. Value pocket identification & quantification what are value pockets?

410. Is this operation cost effective?

411. Why estimate time and cost?

412. What work will be included in the Improve Operation project?

413. What is next?

414. How can the Improve Operation project be displayed graphically to better visualize the activities?

415. What is cost and Improve Operation project cost management?

2.19 Project Schedule: Improve Operation

416. Are all remaining durations correct?

417. To what degree is do you feel the entire team was committed to the Improve Operation project schedule?

418. How much slack is available in the Improve Operation project?

419. Is the Improve Operation project schedule available for all Improve Operation project team members to review?

420. Meet requirements?

421. How do you know that youhave done this right?

422. Verify that the update is accurate. Are all remaining durations correct?

423. What documents, if any, will the subcontractor provide (eg Improve Operation project schedule, quality plan etc)?

424. Change management required?

425. Understand the constraints used in preparing the schedule. Are activities connected because logic dictates the order in which others occur?

426. Why do you think schedule issues often cause the most conflicts on Improve Operation projects?

427. Are activities connected because logic dictates the order in which others occur?

428. The wbs is developed as part of a joint planning session. and how do you know that youhave done this right?

429. Are procedures defined by which the Improve Operation project schedule may be changed?

430. Why or why not?

431. Was the Improve Operation project schedule reviewed by all stakeholders and formally accepted?

432. Is Improve Operation project work proceeding in accordance with the original Improve Operation project schedule?

433. How do you use schedules?

434. Your best shot for providing estimations how complex/how much work does the activity require?

435. What is risk management?

2.20 Cost Management Plan: Improve Operation

436. Are risk triggers captured?

437. Are Improve Operation project team members involved in detailed estimating and scheduling?

438. Is there a formal set of procedures supporting Stakeholder Management?

439. Schedule contingency – how will the schedule contingency be administrated?

440. Have Improve Operation project team accountabilities & responsibilities been clearly defined?

441. Were the budget estimates reasonable?

442. The definition of the Improve Operation project scope what needs to be accomplished?

443. Does the resource management plan include a personnel development plan?

444. Is there anything unique in this Improve Operation projects scope statement that will affect resources?

445. Are risk oriented checklists used during risk identification?

446. Resources – how will human resources be scheduled during each phase of the Improve Operation project?

447. Quality assurance overheads?

448. Is the Improve Operation project schedule available for all Improve Operation project team members to review?

449. Scope of work – What is the likelihood and extent of potential future changes to the Improve Operation project scope?

450. Does the Improve Operation project have a formal Improve Operation project Charter?

451. What is an Acceptance Management Process?

452. Are all vendor contracts closed out?

453. What would the life cycle costs be?

2.21 Activity Cost Estimates: Improve Operation

454. What were things that you did well, and could improve, and how?

455. How many activities should you have?

456. What defines a successful Improve Operation project?

457. When do you enter into PPM?

458. Were decisions made in a timely manner?

459. Measurable - are the targets measurable?

460. Were the costs or charges reasonable?

461. Padding is bad and contingencies are good. what is the difference?

462. If you are asked to lower your estimate because the price is too high, what are your options?

463. What makes a good activity description?

464. What makes a good expected result statement?

465. What cost data should be used to estimate costs during the 2-year follow-up period?

466. Can you change your activities?

467. What is your organizations history in doing similar tasks?

468. Are data needed on characteristics of care?

469. Did the consultant work with local staff to develop local capacity?

470. How do you change activities?

471. What is a Improve Operation project Management Plan?

472. What areas does the group agree are the biggest success on the Improve Operation project?

473. Estimated cost?

2.22 Cost Estimating Worksheet: Improve Operation

474. What happens to any remaining funds not used?

475. What is the purpose of estimating?

476. Who is best positioned to know and assist in identifying corresponding factors?

477. Identify the timeframe necessary to monitor progress and collect data to determine how the selected measure has changed?

478. Ask: are others positioned to know, are others credible, and will others cooperate?

479. Is it feasible to establish a control group arrangement?

480. What additional Improve Operation project(s) could be initiated as a result of this Improve Operation project?

481. Is the Improve Operation project responsive to community need?

482. What is the estimated labor cost today based upon this information?

483. Will the Improve Operation project collaborate with the local community and leverage resources?

484. Can a trend be established from historical performance data on the selected measure and are the criteria for using trend analysis or forecasting methods met?

485. Does the Improve Operation project provide innovative ways for stakeholders to overcome obstacles or deliver better outcomes?

486. What costs are to be estimated?

487. What will others want?

488. How will the results be shared and to whom?

489. What can be included?

2.23 Cost Baseline: Improve Operation

490. Who will use corresponding metrics ?

491. Are you meeting with your team regularly?

492. At which frequency ?

493. How likely is it to go wrong?

494. Have the resources used by the Improve Operation project been reassigned to other units or Improve Operation projects?

495. Has the appropriate access to relevant data and analysis capability been granted?

496. If you sold 10x widgets on a day, what would the affect on profits be?

497. How accurate do cost estimates need to be?

498. Should a more thorough impact analysis be conducted?

499. Does the suggested change request represent a desired enhancement to the products functionality?

500. Why do you manage cost?

501. What is cost and Improve Operation project cost management?

502. Are procedures defined by which the cost baseline may be changed?

503. How fast?

504. Improve Operation project goals -should others be reconsidered?

505. Verify business objectives. Are others appropriate, and well-articulated?

506. Does a process exist for establishing a cost baseline to measure Improve Operation project performance?

507. Have all approved changes to the Improve Operation project requirement been identified and impact on the performance, cost, and schedule baselines documented?

2.24 Quality Management Plan: Improve Operation

508. How are people conducting sampling trained?

509. How will you know that a change is actually an improvement?

510. Are there trends or hot spots?

511. How are changes approved?

512. Who is responsible?

513. Is there a Quality Management Plan?

514. Can the requirements be traced to the appropriate components of the solution, as well as test scripts?

515. Does the system design reflect the requirements?

516. Are there unnecessary steps that are creating bottlenecks and/or causing people to wait?

517. How does your organization manage work to promote cooperation, individual initiative, innovation, flexibility, communications, and knowledge/skill sharing across work units?

518. Meet how often?

519. Has a Improve Operation project

Communications Plan been developed?

520. What is the Quality Management Plan?

521. Can it be done better?

522. How does your organization maintain a safe and healthy work environment?

523. What are the appropriate test methods to be used?

524. Have you eliminated all duplicative tasks or manual efforts, where appropriate?

525. What does it do for you (or to me)?

2.25 Quality Metrics: Improve Operation

526. What level of statistical confidence do you use?

527. What about still open problems?

528. Where did complaints, returns and warranty claims come from?

529. How is it being measured?

530. Are quality metrics defined?

531. Are there any open risk issues?

532. Is there a set of procedures to capture, analyze and act on quality metrics?

533. Is material complete (and does it meet the standards)?

534. How do you know if everyone is trying to improve the right things?

535. Do you stratify metrics by product or site?

536. What do you measure?

537. What method of measurement do you use?

538. Who is willing to lead?

539. What documentation is required?

540. Has risk analysis been adequately reviewed?

541. What metrics do you measure?

542. What happens if you get an abnormal result?

543. Which report did you use to create the data you are submitting?

544. Did the team meet the Improve Operation project success criteria documented in the Quality Metrics Matrix?

2.26 Process Improvement Plan: Improve Operation

545. Purpose of goal: the motive is determined by asking, why do you want to achieve this goal?

546. What personnel are the sponsors for that initiative?

547. How do you manage quality?

548. Has the time line required to move measurement results from the points of collection to databases or users been established?

549. Does explicit definition of the measures exist?

550. Where do you focus?

551. What is the return on investment?

552. Modeling current processes is great, and will you ever see a return on that investment?

553. Have storage and access mechanisms and procedures been determined?

554. Are you making progress on the goals?

555. Are there forms and procedures to collect and record the data?

556. Have the frequency of collection and the points

in the process where measurements will be made been determined?

557. Are you meeting the quality standards?

558. Does your process ensure quality?

559. Where do you want to be?

560. What personnel are the coaches for your initiative?

561. Are you making progress on the improvement framework?

562. Why quality management?

563. What personnel are the change agents for your initiative?

2.27 Responsibility Assignment Matrix: Improve Operation

564. What is the number one predictor of a groups productivity?

565. What expertise is available in your department?

566. Do others have the time to dedicate to your Improve Operation project?

567. The already stated responsible for the establishment of budgets and assignment of resources for overhead performance?

568. Not any rs, as, or cs: if an identified role is only informed, should others be eliminated from the matrix?

569. Identify and isolate causes of favorable and unfavorable cost and schedule variances?

570. Are people afraid to let you know when others are under allocated?

571. Are work packages assigned to performing organizations?

572. What are the assumptions?

573. What are some important Improve Operation project communications management tools?

574. Do all the identified groups or people really need to be consulted?

575. Undistributed budgets, if any?

576. Is every signing-off responsibility and every communicating responsibility critically necessary?

577. Is the entire contract planned in time-phased control accounts to the extent practicable?

578. Are records maintained to show how management reserves are used?

579. What do people write/say on status/Improve Operation project reports?

580. Past experience – the person or the group worked at something similar in the past?

581. How many people do you need?

582. What will the work cost?

583. Are there any drawbacks to using a responsibility assignment matrix?

2.28 Roles and Responsibilities: Improve Operation

584. What specific behaviors did you observe?

585. To decide whether to use a quality measurement, ask how will you know when it is achieved?

586. Implementation of actions: Who are the responsible units?

587. What should you highlight for improvement?

588. What is working well within your organizations performance management system?

589. What expectations were met?

590. Who is involved?

591. Where are you most strong as a supervisor?

592. What is working well?

593. How well did the Improve Operation project Team understand the expectations of specific roles and responsibilities?

594. What should you do now to ensure that you are meeting all expectations of your current position?

595. Is feedback clearly communicated and non-judgmental?

596. Who is responsible for each task?

597. Once the responsibilities are defined for the Improve Operation project, have the deliverables, roles and responsibilities been clearly communicated to every participant?

598. Who: who is involved?

599. Are Improve Operation project team roles and responsibilities identified and documented?

600. Required skills, knowledge, experience?

601. Key conclusions and recommendations: Are conclusions and recommendations relevant and acceptable?

602. Are governance roles and responsibilities documented?

2.29 Human Resource Management Plan: Improve Operation

603. Is the manpower level sufficient to meet the future business requirements?

604. Are multiple estimation methods being employed?

605. What were things that you need to improve?

606. Does the Improve Operation project have a Quality Culture?

607. Were Improve Operation project team members involved in the development of activity & task decomposition?

608. Are mitigation strategies identified?

609. Is the assigned Improve Operation project manager a PMP (Certified Improve Operation project manager) and experienced?

610. Are target dates established for each milestone deliverable?

611. Have the procedures for identifying budget variances been followed?

612. Who will be impacted (both positively and negatively) as a result of or during the execution of this Improve Operation project?

613. Was the scope definition used in task sequencing?

614. Were escalated issues resolved promptly?

615. Are enough systems & user personnel assigned to the Improve Operation project?

616. Has the Improve Operation project manager been identified?

617. Is the current culture aligned with the vision, mission, and values of the department?

618. Are there checklists created to determine if all quality processes are followed?

619. Is the schedule updated on a periodic basis?

620. Improve Operation project definition & scope?

2.30 Communications Management Plan: Improve Operation

621. Do you prepare stakeholder engagement plans?

622. Why do you manage communications?

623. Do you then often overlook a key stakeholder or stakeholder group?

624. Are there too many who have an interest in some aspect of your work?

625. Who have you worked with in past, similar initiatives?

626. Do you ask; can you recommend others for you to talk with about this initiative?

627. How often do you engage with stakeholders?

628. Are there common objectives between the team and the stakeholder?

629. Timing: when do the effects of the communication take place?

630. Who to learn from?

631. Are others part of the communications management plan?

632. Where do team members get information?

633. Are there potential barriers between the team and the stakeholder?

634. Are you constantly rushing from meeting to meeting?

635. What is the political influence?

636. How is this initiative related to other portfolios, programs, or Improve Operation projects?

637. Why is stakeholder engagement important?

638. In your work, how much time is spent on stakeholder identification?

639. Which stakeholders can influence others?

640. Who did you turn to if you had questions?

2.31 Risk Management Plan: Improve Operation

641. Are you on schedule?

642. Is a software Improve Operation project management tool available?

643. Does the Improve Operation project have the authority and ability to avoid the risk?

644. What can you do to minimize the impact if it does?

645. Which is an input to the risk management process?

646. Are the reports useful and easy to read?

647. Are certain activities taking a long time to complete?

648. Internal technical and management reviews?

649. Do end-users have realistic expectations?

650. Is the process being followed?

651. Does the Improve Operation project team have experience with the technology to be implemented?

652. What risks are necessary to achieve success?

653. Are people attending meetings and doing work?

654. Which risks should get the attention?

655. Could others have been better mitigated?

656. How is the audit profession changing?

657. Are the software tools integrated with each other?

658. Are the best people available?

659. Is there anything you would now do differently on your Improve Operation project based on this experience?

660. Is the process supported by tools?

2.32 Risk Register: Improve Operation

661. Manageability – have mitigations to the risk been identified?

662. Which key risks have ineffective responses or outstanding improvement actions?

663. Contingency actions - planned actions to reduce the immediate seriousness of the risk when it does occur. What should you do when?

664. Who needs to know about this?

665. What is a Community Risk Register?

666. Have other controls and solutions been implemented in other services which could be applied as an alternative to additional funding?

667. Technology risk -is the Improve Operation project technically feasible?

668. Risk documentation: what reporting formats and processes will be used for risk management activities?

669. What would the impact to the Improve Operation project objectives be should the risk arise?

670. Preventative actions - planned actions to reduce the likelihood a risk will occur and/or reduce the seriousness should it occur. What should you do now?

671. What evidence do you have to justify the

likelihood score of the risk (audit, incident report, claim, complaints, inspection, internal review)?

672. Are there other alternative controls that could be implemented?

673. How are risks graded?

674. What can be done about it?

675. Are there any gaps in the evidence?

676. What is the appropriate level of risk management for this Improve Operation project?

677. What are the main aims, objectives of the policy, strategy, or service and the intended outcomes?

678. How are risks identified?

679. Severity Prediction?

2.33 Probability and Impact Assessment: Improve Operation

680. Are the risk data timely and relevant?

681. Do you use any methods to analyze risks?

682. Are tool mentors available?

683. What are the chances the event will occur?

684. Anticipated volatility of the requirements?

685. How is risk handled within this Improve Operation project organization?

686. What things might go wrong?

687. How do the products attain the specifications?

688. What are the tools and techniques used in managing the challenges faced?

689. Do you have specific methods that you use for each phase of the process?

690. Are there new risks that mitigation strategies might introduce?

691. Are some people working on multiple Improve Operation projects?

692. Are there alternative opinions/solutions/

processes you should explore?

693. What should be the requirement of organizational restructuring as each subImprove Operation project goes through a different lifecycle phase?

694. Are requirements fully understood by the software engineering team and customers?

695. What will be the likely political situation during the life of the Improve Operation project?

696. Are tools for analysis and design available?

697. Are the risk data complete?

2.34 Probability and Impact Matrix: Improve Operation

698. Why do you need to manage Improve Operation project Risk?

699. What has the Improve Operation project manager forgotten to do?

700. What will be cost of redeployment of the personnel?

701. Were there any Improve Operation projects similar to this one in existence?

702. Are staff committed for the duration of the Improve Operation project?

703. Can you handle the investment risk?

704. What risks were tracked?

705. Does the customer understand the software process?

706. What is the risk appetite?

707. Have you worked with the customer in the past?

708. Who are the owners?

709. Risk may be made during which step of risk management?

710. Which risks need to move on to Perform Quantitative Risk Analysis?

711. Are you working on the right risks?

712. How do you manage Improve Operation project Risk?

713. What is the probability of the risk occurring?

714. Do the people have the right combinations of skills?

2.35 Risk Data Sheet: Improve Operation

715. Whom do you serve (customers)?

716. Has the most cost-effective solution been chosen?

717. What will be the consequences if the risk happens?

718. What was measured?

719. What actions can be taken to eliminate or remove risk?

720. What are your core values?

721. Risk of what?

722. Has a sensitivity analysis been carried out?

723. Are new hazards created?

724. What is the environment within which you operate (social trends, economic, community values, broad based participation, national directions etc.)?

725. What can happen?

726. What are the main opportunities available to you that you should grab while you can?

727. What were the Causes that contributed?

728. What are you trying to achieve (Objectives)?

729. What are you here for (Mission)?

730. How can hazards be reduced?

731. What is the likelihood of it happening?

732. Is the data sufficiently specified in terms of the type of failure being analyzed, and its frequency or probability?

733. What will be the consequences if it happens?

734. What are you weak at and therefore need to do better?

2.36 Procurement Management Plan: Improve Operation

735. Is stakeholder involvement adequate?

736. How will the duration of the Improve Operation project influence your decisions?

737. Specific - is the objective clear in terms of what, how, when, and where the situation will be changed?

738. Has your organization readiness assessment been conducted?

739. Are milestone deliverables effectively tracked and compared to Improve Operation project plan?

740. Were Improve Operation project team members involved in the development of activity & task decomposition?

741. How will you coordinate Procurement with aspects of the Improve Operation project?

742. Financial capacity; does the seller have, or can the seller reasonably be expected to obtain, the financial resources needed?

743. Are metrics used to evaluate and manage Vendors?

744. Is Improve Operation project work proceeding in accordance with the original Improve Operation

project schedule?

745. In which phase of the Acquisition Process Cycle does source qualifications reside?

746. Are software metrics formally captured, analyzed and used as a basis for other Improve Operation project estimates?

747. Are the payment terms being followed?

748. What types of contracts will be used?

749. Are parking lot items captured?

2.37 Source Selection Criteria: Improve Operation

750. Are there any common areas of weaknesses or deficiencies in the proposals in the competitive range?

751. What is price analysis and when should it be performed?

752. How important is cost in the source selection decision relative to past performance and technical considerations?

753. Can you reasonably estimate total organization requirements for the coming year?

754. How can solicitation Schedules be improved to yield more effective price competition?

755. Is the contracting office likely to receive more purchase requests for this item or service during the coming year?

756. What should be considered?

757. In the technical/management area, what criteria do you use to determine the final evaluation ratings?

758. Are types/quantities of material, facilities appropriate?

759. Do you want to have them collaborate at

subfactor level?

760. How are clarifications and communications appropriately used?

761. Team leads: what is your process for assigning ratings?

762. What source selection software is your team using?

763. When is it appropriate to issue a DRFP?

764. Who should attend debriefings?

765. How is past performance evaluated?

766. What instructions should be provided regarding oral presentations?

767. Who is on the Source Selection Advisory Committee?

768. How should the oral presentations be handled?

2.38 Stakeholder Management Plan: Improve Operation

769. Do any protocols apply for records management?

770. Are you meeting your customers expectations consistently?

771. Are vendor invoices audited for accuracy before payment?

772. Describe the process that will be used to design, develop, review, accept, distribute and change outputs. Will all outputs delivered by the Improve Operation project follow the same process?

773. Have all involved Improve Operation project stakeholders and work groups committed to the Improve Operation project?

774. How is information analyzed, and what specific pieces of data would be of interest to the Improve Operation project manager?

775. Are formal code reviews conducted?

776. What has to be purchased?

777. Is a payment system in place with proper reviews and approvals?

778. Are the people assigned to the Improve Operation project sufficiently qualified?

779. Do you know what your customers expectations are regarding this process?

780. Has the business need been clearly defined?

781. What are the criteria for selecting suppliers of off the shelf products?

782. Is the Improve Operation project sponsor clearly communicating the business case or rationale for why this Improve Operation project is needed?

783. Has the scope management document been updated and distributed to help prevent scope creep?

784. What guidelines or procedures currently exist that must be adhered to (eg departmental accounting procedures)?

2.39 Change Management Plan: Improve Operation

785. What tasks are needed?

786. When does it make sense to customize?

787. What skills, education, knowledge, or work experiences should the resources have for each identified competency?

788. What are the specific target groups / audience that will be impacted by this change?

789. Will the readiness criteria be met prior to the training roll out?

790. Clearly articulate the overall business benefits of the Improve Operation project -why are you doing this now?

791. What prerequisite knowledge or training is required?

792. Where will the funds come from?

793. How much change management is needed?

794. Will you need new processes?

795. Has the training provider been established?

796. Do you need a new organization structure?

797. What are the major changes to processes?

798. What would be an estimate of the total cost for the activities required to carry out the change initiative?

799. Do you need new systems?

800. Do you need a new organizational structure?

801. What are the training strategies?

802. What is going to be done differently?

803. What risks may occur upfront?

804. Has the training co-ordinator been provided with the training details and put in place the necessary arrangements?

3.0 Executing Process Group: Improve Operation

805. Will new hardware or software be required for servers or client machines?

806. Do your results resemble a normal distribution?

807. How do you prevent staff are just doing busywork to pass the time?

808. What are the Improve Operation project management deliverables of each process group?

809. If action is called for, what form should it take?

810. What is in place for ensuring adequate change control on Improve Operation projects that involve outside contracts?

811. How well did the team follow the chosen processes?

812. Why should Improve Operation project managers strive to make jobs look easy?

813. What does it mean to take a systems view of a Improve Operation project?

814. Who will provide training?

815. When will the Improve Operation project be done?

816. What is the critical path for this Improve Operation project and how long is it?

817. Is the schedule for the set products being met?

818. How will you know you did it?

819. Why is it important to determine activity sequencing on Improve Operation projects?

820. How will you avoid scope creep?

821. After how many days will the lease cost be the same as the purchase cost for the equipment?

822. What is the shortest possible time it will take to complete this Improve Operation project?

823. What are the critical steps involved with strategy mapping?

824. What good practices or successful experiences or transferable examples have been identified?

3.1 Team Member Status Report: Improve Operation

825. What is to be done?

826. How can you make it practical?

827. Does every department have to have a Improve Operation project Manager on staff?

828. Does your organization have the means (staff, money, contract, etc.) to produce or to acquire the product, good, or service?

829. When a teams productivity and success depend on collaboration and the efficient flow of information, what generally fails them?

830. How much risk is involved?

831. Will the staff do training or is that done by a third party?

832. Do you have an Enterprise Improve Operation project Management Office (EPMO)?

833. How will resource planning be done?

834. How it is to be done?

835. Does the product, good, or service already exist within your organization?

836. Are your organizations Improve Operation projects more successful over time?

837. Are the attitudes of staff regarding Improve Operation project work improving?

838. The problem with Reward & Recognition Programs is that the truly deserving people all too often get left out. How can you make it practical?

839. Is there evidence that staff is taking a more professional approach toward management of your organizations Improve Operation projects?

840. How does this product, good, or service meet the needs of the Improve Operation project and your organization as a whole?

841. What specific interest groups do you have in place?

842. Why is it to be done?

843. Are the products of your organizations Improve Operation projects meeting customers objectives?

3.2 Change Request: Improve Operation

844. How do you get changes (code) out in a timely manner?

845. What mechanism is used to appraise others of changes that are made?

846. Will all change requests and current status be logged?

847. For which areas does this operating procedure apply?

848. Can you answer what happened, who did it, when did it happen, and what else will be affected?

849. Who is responsible to authorize changes?

850. Since there are no change requests in your Improve Operation project at this point, what must you have before you begin?

851. Where do changes come from?

852. How well do experienced software developers predict software change?

853. How shall the implementation of changes be recorded?

854. Who needs to approve change requests?

855. Why do you want to have a change control system?

856. Will the change use memory to the extent that other functions will be not have sufficient memory to operate effectively?

857. What is a Change Request Form?

858. Have scm procedures for noting the change, recording it, and reporting it been followed?

859. What is the function of the change control committee?

860. What should be regulated in a change control operating instruction?

861. How do team members communicate with each other?

862. What are the requirements for urgent changes?

863. What is the relationship between requirements attributes and attributes like complexity and size?

3.3 Change Log: Improve Operation

864. How does this change affect the timeline of the schedule?

865. Do the described changes impact on the integrity or security of the system?

866. Is the submitted change a new change or a modification of a previously approved change?

867. Is this a mandatory replacement?

868. How does this relate to the standards developed for specific business processes?

869. Will the Improve Operation project fail if the change request is not executed?

870. Is the change backward compatible without limitations?

871. How does this change affect scope?

872. Does the suggested change request seem to represent a necessary enhancement to the product?

873. Is the change request within Improve Operation project scope?

874. Who initiated the change request?

875. When was the request approved?

876. Is the requested change request a result of changes in other Improve Operation project(s)?

877. When was the request submitted?

878. Is the change request open, closed or pending?

3.4 Decision Log: Improve Operation

879. How do you define success?

880. What is your overall strategy for quality control / quality assurance procedures?

881. Linked to original objective?

882. With whom was the decision shared or considered?

883. What alternatives/risks were considered?

884. Which variables make a critical difference?

885. Behaviors; what are guidelines that the team has identified that will assist them with getting the most out of team meetings?

886. What are the cost implications?

887. How does an increasing emphasis on cost containment influence the strategies and tactics used?

888. Is your opponent open to a non-traditional workflow, or will it likely challenge anything you do?

889. What was the rationale for the decision?

890. At what point in time does loss become unacceptable?

891. It becomes critical to track and periodically revisit both operational effectiveness; Are you noticing all that you need to, and are you interpreting what you see effectively?

892. How effective is maintaining the log at facilitating organizational learning?

893. What eDiscovery problem or issue did your organization set out to fix or make better?

894. How do you know when you are achieving it?

895. What is the line where eDiscovery ends and document review begins?

896. Is everything working as expected?

897. What makes you different or better than others companies selling the same thing?

898. Who is the decisionmaker?

3.5 Quality Audit: Improve Operation

899. How do you indicate the extent to which your personnel would be expected to contribute to the work effort?

900. How does your organization know that its staff have appropriate access to a fair and effective grievance process?

901. What data about organizational performance is routinely collected and reported?

902. Does everyone know what they are supposed to be doing, how and why?

903. How does your organization know that its Strategic Plan is providing the best guidance for the future of your organization?

904. Are the intentions consistent with external obligations (such as applicable laws)?

905. Are all staff empowered and encouraged to contribute to ongoing improvement efforts?

906. How does your organization know that its system for ensuring a positive organizational climate is appropriately effective and constructive?

907. Are storage areas and reconditioning operations designed to prevent mix-ups and assure orderly handling of both the distressed and reconditioned devices?

908. What are you trying to accomplish with this audit?

909. How does your organization know that its range of activities are being reviewed as rigorously and constructively as they could be?

910. Is your organizational structure established and each positions responsibility defined?

911. How does your organization know that its systems for providing high quality consultancy services to external parties are appropriately effective and constructive?

912. How does your organization know that its management system is appropriately effective and constructive?

913. How does your organization know that its system for attending to the particular needs of its international staff is appropriately effective and constructive?

914. How does your organization know that its system for recruiting the best staff possible are appropriately effective and constructive?

915. How does your organization know that its teaching activities (and staff learning) are effectively and constructively enhanced by its activities?

916. Why are you trying to do it?

917. How does your organization know that its

general support services planning and management systems are appropriately effective and constructive?

918. How does your organization know that its processes for managing severance are appropriately effective, constructive and fair?

3.6 Team Directory: Improve Operation

919. Is construction on schedule?

920. Process decisions: are all start-up, turn over and close out requirements of the contract satisfied?

921. Process decisions: how well was task order work performed?

922. Who are your stakeholders (customers, sponsors, end users, team members)?

923. Decisions: is the most suitable form of contract being used?

924. Does a Improve Operation project team directory list all resources assigned to the Improve Operation project?

925. Who will be the stakeholders on your next Improve Operation project?

926. Who are the Team Members?

927. Contract requirements complied with?

928. How will the team handle changes?

929. How do unidentified risks impact the outcome of the Improve Operation project?

930. Who will talk to the customer?

931. What needs to be communicated?

932. Who will report Improve Operation project status to all stakeholders?

933. Process decisions: do invoice amounts match accepted work in place?

934. Where should the information be distributed?

935. Who will write the meeting minutes and distribute?

936. Do purchase specifications and configurations match requirements?

937. How and in what format should information be presented?

3.7 Team Operating Agreement: Improve Operation

938. How will you resolve conflict efficiently and respectfully?

939. Do you brief absent members after they view meeting notes or listen to a recording?

940. Do team members need to frequently communicate as a full group to make timely decisions?

941. Do you ensure that all participants know how to use the required technology?

942. To whom do you deliver your services?

943. What are the current caseload numbers in the unit?

944. Do you determine the meeting length and time of day?

945. Do you prevent individuals from dominating the meeting?

946. Are there the right people on your team?

947. What administrative supports will be put in place to support the team and the teams supervisor?

948. Methodologies: how will key team processes

be implemented, such as training, research, work deliverable production, review and approval processes, knowledge management, and meeting procedures?

949. Are there more than two national cultures represented by your team?

950. What is the number of cases currently teamed?

951. Conflict resolution: how will disputes and other conflicts be mediated or resolved?

952. Do you send out the agenda and meeting materials in advance?

953. Do you vary your voice pace, tone and pitch to engage participants and gain involvement?

954. What is a Virtual Team?

955. What is your unique contribution to your organization?

956. Do you record meetings for the already stated unable to attend?

3.8 Team Performance Assessment: Improve Operation

957. How do you keep key people outside the group informed about its accomplishments?

958. Does more radicalness mean more perceived benefits?

959. To what degree are the skill areas critical to team performance present?

960. To what degree will the team ensure that all members equitably share the work essential to the success of the team?

961. What are you doing specifically to develop the leaders around you?

962. To what degree will team members, individually and collectively, commit time to help themselves and others learn and develop skills?

963. To what degree are sub-teams possible or necessary?

964. How hard do you try to make a good selection?

965. To what degree are the relative importance and priority of the goals clear to all team members?

966. Do friends perform better than acquaintances?

967. Do you promptly inform members about major developments that may affect them?

968. To what degree can team members vigorously define the teams purpose in considerations with others who are not part of the functioning team?

969. To what degree are the teams goals and objectives clear, simple, and measurable?

970. How do you recognize and praise members for contributions?

971. Social categorization and intergroup behaviour: Does minimal intergroup discrimination make social identity more positive?

972. To what degree are staff involved as partners in the improvement process?

973. If you have received criticism from reviewers that your work suffered from method variance, what was the circumstance?

974. To what degree does the teams work approach provide opportunity for members to engage in fact-based problem solving?

975. To what degree does the teams purpose constitute a broader, deeper aspiration than just accomplishing short-term goals?

976. To what degree do team members agree with the goals, relative importance, and the ways in which achievement will be measured?

3.9 Team Member Performance Assessment: Improve Operation

977. To what degree is there a sense that only the team can succeed?

978. To what degree can the team measure progress against specific goals?

979. What are the staffs preferences for training on technology-based platforms?

980. To what degree do team members feel that the purpose of the team is important, if not exciting?

981. What are top priorities?

982. What types of learning are targeted (e.g., cognitive, affective, psychomotor, procedural)?

983. What evidence supports your decision-making?

984. Are the draft goals SMART ?

985. Verify business objectives. Are they appropriate, and well-articulated?

986. How will you identify your Team Leaders?

987. Is it critical or vital to the job?

988. What is collaboration?

989. For what period of time is a member rated?

990. What are best practices in use for the performance measurement system?

991. What stakeholders must be involved in the development and oversight of the performance plan?

992. Does adaptive training work?

993. How should adaptive assessments be implemented?

994. What kinds of performance factors / elements do you use?

3.10 Issue Log: Improve Operation

995. Why multiple evaluators?

996. How do you manage communications?

997. Do you have members of your team responsible for certain stakeholders?

998. Do you feel a register helps?

999. Who do you turn to if you have questions?

1000. What would have to change?

1001. What approaches to you feel are the best ones to use?

1002. Do you often overlook a key stakeholder or stakeholder group?

1003. What is a Stakeholder?

1004. What date was the issue resolved?

1005. Who is the stakeholder?

1006. What are the typical contents?

1007. Is the issue log kept in a safe place?

1008. How much time does it take to do it?

1009. Persistence; will users learn a work around or

will they be bothered every time?

1010. Who reported the issue?

1011. What is the impact on the risks?

1012. Are the stakeholders getting the information they need, are they consulted, are concerns addressed?

4.0 Monitoring and Controlling Process Group: Improve Operation

1013. How to ensure validity, quality and consistency?

1014. How is Agile Improve Operation project Management done?

1015. What are the goals of the program?

1016. What do they need to know about the Improve Operation project?

1017. How is agile Improve Operation project management done?

1018. Key stakeholders to work with. How many potential communications channels exist on the Improve Operation project?

1019. Is the program making progress in helping to achieve the set results?

1020. How were collaborations developed, and how are they sustained?

1021. Is progress on outcomes due to your program?

1022. What resources are necessary?

1023. How is agile program management done?

1024. Is there adequate validation on required fields?

1025. How do you monitor progress?

1026. How well did the chosen processes produce the expected results?

1027. What input will you be required to provide the Improve Operation project team?

1028. What is the expected monetary value of the Improve Operation project?

1029. Did you implement the program as designed?

1030. Does the solution fit in with organizations technical architectural requirements?

1031. How well did the chosen processes fit the needs of the Improve Operation project?

1032. Mitigate. what will you do to minimize the impact should a risk event occur?

4.1 Project Performance Report: Improve Operation

1033. To what degree are fresh input and perspectives systematically caught and added (for example, through information and analysis, new members, and senior sponsors)?

1034. To what degree is the information network consistent with the structure of the formal organization?

1035. To what degree does the informal organization make use of individual resources and meet individual needs?

1036. To what degree do all members feel responsible for all agreed-upon measures?

1037. To what degree can all members engage in open and interactive considerations?

1038. To what degree are the goals realistic?

1039. To what degree do the structures of the formal organization motivate taskrelevant behavior and facilitate task completion?

1040. To what degree does the teams work approach provide opportunity for members to engage in results-based evaluation?

1041. To what degree does the funding match the

requirement?

1042. To what degree does the teams approach to its work allow for modification and improvement over time?

1043. Next Steps?

1044. To what degree can the cognitive capacity of individuals accommodate the flow of information?

1045. To what degree do team members understand one anothers roles and skills?

1046. To what degree does the teams work approach provide opportunity for members to engage in open interaction?

1047. To what degree will each member have the opportunity to advance his or her professional skills in all three of the above categories while contributing to the accomplishment of the teams purpose and goals?

1048. How will procurement be coordinated with other Improve Operation project aspects, such as scheduling and performance reporting?

4.2 Variance Analysis: Improve Operation

1049. What business event causes fluctuations?

1050. Are control accounts opened and closed based on the start and completion of work contained therein?

1051. Did a new competitor enter the market?

1052. How have the setting and use of standards changed over time?

1053. What should management do?

1054. How do you manage changes in the nature of the overhead requirements?

1055. Do the rates and prices remain constant throughout the year?

1056. Wbs elements contractually specified for reporting of status to your organization (lowest level only)?

1057. How are material, labor, and overhead variances calculated and recorded?

1058. Are procedures for variance analysis documented and consistently applied at the control account level and selected WBS and organizational levels at least monthly as a routine task?

1059. Is there a logical explanation for any variance?

1060. What was the cause of the increase in costs?

1061. Is cost and schedule performance measurement done in a consistent, systematic manner?

1062. Are the overhead pools formally and adequately identified?

1063. What is exceptional?

1064. Is the anticipated (firm and potential) business base Improve Operation projected in a rational, consistent manner?

1065. Did your organization lose existing customers and/or gain new customers?

1066. Are the requirements for all items of overhead established by rational, traceable processes?

4.3 Earned Value Status: Improve Operation

1067. Are you hitting your Improve Operation projects targets?

1068. Where is evidence-based earned value in your organization reported?

1069. How much is it going to cost by the finish?

1070. Verification is a process of ensuring that the developed system satisfies the stakeholders agreements and specifications; Are you building the product right? What do you verify?

1071. Where are your problem areas?

1072. What is the unit of forecast value?

1073. If earned value management (EVM) is so good in determining the true status of a Improve Operation project and Improve Operation project its completion, why is it that hardly any one uses it in information systems related Improve Operation projects?

1074. Validation is a process of ensuring that the developed system will actually achieve the stakeholders desired outcomes; Are you building the right product? What do you validate?

1075. When is it going to finish?

1076. How does this compare with other Improve Operation projects?

1077. Earned value can be used in almost any Improve Operation project situation and in almost any Improve Operation project environment. it may be used on large Improve Operation projects, medium sized Improve Operation projects, tiny Improve Operation projects (in cut-down form), complex and simple Improve Operation projects and in any market sector. some people, of course, know all about earned value, they have used it for years - but perhaps not as effectively as they could have?

4.4 Risk Audit: Improve Operation

1078. Have risks been considered with an insurance broker or provider and suitable insurance cover been arranged?

1079. Where will the next scandal or adverse media involving your organization come from?

1080. What are the costs associated with late delivery or a defective product?

1081. Will an appropriate standard of care be applied to all involved?

1082. Do you have a mechanism for managing change?

1083. Does your organization meet the terms of any contracts with which it is involved?

1084. Do you meet all obligations relating to funds secured from grants, loans and sponsors?

1085. Is the customer willing to participate in reviews?

1086. Level of preparation and skill?

1087. What resources are needed to achieve program results?

1088. Have staff received necessary training?

1089. Should additional substantive testing be

conducted because of the risk audit results?

1090. Is your organization willing to commit significant time to the requirements gathering process?

1091. Are audit program plans risk-adjusted?

1092. Is a software Improve Operation project management tool available?

1093. Will safety checks of personal equipment supplied by competitors be conducted?

1094. What are the strategic implications with clients when auditors focus audit resources based on business-level risks?

1095. Have all possible risks/hazards been identified (including injury to staff, damage to equipment, impact on others in the community)?

1096. Do you have a procedure for dealing with complaints?

4.5 Contractor Status Report: Improve Operation

1097. Who can list a Improve Operation project as organization experience, your organization or a previous employee of your organization?

1098. What was the overall budget or estimated cost?

1099. If applicable; describe your standard schedule for new software version releases. Are new software version releases included in the standard maintenance plan?

1100. How long have you been using the services?

1101. Are there contractual transfer concerns?

1102. What process manages the contracts?

1103. What was the budget or estimated cost for your organizations services?

1104. What was the final actual cost?

1105. What was the actual budget or estimated cost for your organizations services?

1106. How is risk transferred?

1107. What is the average response time for answering a support call?

1108. How does the proposed individual meet each requirement?

1109. What are the minimum and optimal bandwidth requirements for the proposed solution?

1110. Describe how often regular updates are made to the proposed solution. Are corresponding regular updates included in the standard maintenance plan?

4.6 Formal Acceptance: Improve Operation

1111. Was the Improve Operation project work done on time, within budget, and according to specification?

1112. What was done right?

1113. Have all comments been addressed?

1114. What are the requirements against which to test, Who will execute?

1115. Was the sponsor/customer satisfied?

1116. How well did the team follow the methodology?

1117. What lessons were learned about your Improve Operation project management methodology?

1118. Who supplies data?

1119. Do you buy-in installation services?

1120. Was the Improve Operation project managed well?

1121. Was the client satisfied with the Improve Operation project results?

1122. Do you perform formal acceptance or burn-in tests?

1123. Does it do what Improve Operation project team said it would?

1124. What function(s) does it fill or meet?

1125. Do you buy pre-configured systems or build your own configuration?

1126. How does your team plan to obtain formal acceptance on your Improve Operation project?

1127. General estimate of the costs and times to complete the Improve Operation project?

1128. Who would use it?

1129. Is formal acceptance of the Improve Operation project product documented and distributed?

1130. Was the Improve Operation project goal achieved?

5.0 Closing Process Group: Improve Operation

1131. What is the overall risk of the Improve Operation project to your organization?

1132. How will staff learn how to use the deliverables?

1133. Did the Improve Operation project management methodology work?

1134. Did the delivered product meet the specified requirements and goals of the Improve Operation project?

1135. Was the schedule met?

1136. Did you do what you said you were going to do?

1137. What is an Encumbrance?

1138. Based on your Improve Operation project communication management plan, what worked well?

1139. Are there funding or time constraints?

1140. What communication items need improvement?

1141. What business situation is being addressed?

1142. Is there a clear cause and effect between the

activity and the lesson learned?

1143. What will you do?

1144. What was learned?

5.1 Procurement Audit: Improve Operation

1145. Could bidders learn all relevant information straight from the tender documents?

1146. Were there no material changes in the contract shortly after award?

1147. Did the contracting authority draw up a comprehensive written report about progress and outcome of the procurement process?

1148. Are individuals with check-signing responsibility prohibited from signing blank checks?

1149. How is the evaluation of contract performance organized?

1150. How do you assess whether the technical and financial evaluation was done properly and in fair manner?

1151. Is the purchasing department facility laid out to facilitate interviews with salespersons?

1152. Are there systems for recording and managing stocks (where part of contract)?

1153. Does each policy statement contain the legal reference(s) on which the policy is based?

1154. Are all purchase orders cancelled after payment

to avoid duplicate payment of the same invoice?

1155. Are controls proportionated to risks?

1156. Is a risk evaluation performed?

1157. Does your organization have an overall procurement strategy and/or policy?

1158. Were the documents received scrutinised for completion and adherence to stated conditions before the tenders were evaluated?

1159. Are the purchase order forms designed for efficient and simple completion?

1160. Are the responsibilities of the purchasing department clearly defined?

1161. Are internal control mechanisms performed before payments?

1162. Has your organization taken a well-grounded decision about the procurement procedure chosen and has it documented the process?

1163. Were the tender documents comprehensive, transparent and non-discriminating?

1164. Is there a form specified for bids?

5.2 Contract Close-Out: Improve Operation

1165. What is capture management?

1166. Change in knowledge?

1167. Was the contract complete without requiring numerous changes and revisions?

1168. Parties: Authorized?

1169. How/when used ?

1170. How does it work?

1171. Change in circumstances?

1172. How is the contracting office notified of the automatic contract close-out?

1173. Have all contracts been closed?

1174. What happens to the recipient of services?

1175. Has each contract been audited to verify acceptance and delivery?

1176. Change in attitude or behavior?

1177. Are the signers the authorized officials?

1178. Why Outsource?

1179. Have all contracts been completed?

1180. Have all contract records been included in the Improve Operation project archives?

1181. Parties: who is involved?

1182. Was the contract sufficiently clear so as not to result in numerous disputes and misunderstandings?

1183. Have all acceptance criteria been met prior to final payment to contractors?

1184. Was the contract type appropriate?

5.3 Project or Phase Close-Out: Improve Operation

1185. How often did each stakeholder need an update?

1186. What were the goals and objectives of the communications strategy for the Improve Operation project?

1187. Who exerted influence that has positively affected or negatively impacted the Improve Operation project?

1188. What advantages do the an individual interview have over a group meeting, and vice-versa?

1189. When and how were information needs best met?

1190. Were risks identified and mitigated?

1191. Did the Improve Operation project management methodology work?

1192. What was expected from each stakeholder?

1193. What is in it for you?

1194. What is a Risk?

1195. What stakeholder group needs, expectations, and interests are being met by the Improve Operation project?

1196. What were the actual outcomes?

1197. Does the lesson describe a function that would be done differently the next time?

1198. What are the marketing communication needs for each stakeholder?

1199. What information did each stakeholder need to contribute to the Improve Operation projects success?

1200. Which changes might a stakeholder be required to make as a result of the Improve Operation project?

1201. How much influence did the stakeholder have over others?

1202. Complete yes or no?

1203. What is this stakeholder expecting?

5.4 Lessons Learned: Improve Operation

1204. Were any strategies or activities unsuccessful?

1205. What are the needs of the individuals?

1206. How much communication is socially oriented?

1207. How well is the build process working?

1208. What is (are) the indicator(s) of success?

1209. How effective was Improve Operation project Team member training?

1210. Will the information remain current?

1211. How much of your time was spent on other than this Improve Operation project?

1212. What worked well or did not work well, either for this Improve Operation project or for the Improve Operation project team?

1213. What on the Improve Operation project worked well and was effective in the delivery of the product?

1214. Was the purpose of the Improve Operation project, the end products and success criteria clearly defined and agreed at the start?

1215. What was the geopolitical history during the

origin of your organization and at the time of task input?

1216. How did the estimated Improve Operation project Budget compare with the total actual expenditures?

1217. What would you like to see better documented about how to use existing processes on this type of Improve Operation project?

1218. How effective was the training you received in preparation for the use of the product/service?

1219. What are the funding priorities for intelligence?

1220. How well did the Improve Operation project Manager respond to questions or comments related to the Improve Operation project?

1221. How many government and contractor personnel are authorized for the Improve Operation project?

1222. What are the external dependencies?

Index

CPSIA information can be obtained
at www.ICGtesting.com
Printed in the USA
BVHW042306280719
554530BV00014B/947/P